THE DORSET AND SOMERSET REBELLION

G000154590

K. MERLE CHACKSFIELD

Dorset Publishing Company, Knock-na-cre
Milborne Port, Sherborne, Dorset DT9 5HJ

dpc

Acknowledgements

I am grateful to the following for their valuable help in the preparation of this book:-

The National Portrait Gallery for permission to use Kneller's Portrait of James, Duke of Monmouth.

The Librarian, Miss P. C. Williams A.L.A. and the Staff of the Swanage Branch of the Dorset County Library Service.

Mrs. Jean Mattravers, The Sedgemoor Inn, Weston Zoyland, Somerset.

The staff of Judge Jeffreys' Restaurant, Dorchester, Dorset.

Mrs. Jenny Teague, The Antelope Hotel, Dorchester, Dorset.

Mr. Stephen Minnitt, Senior Keeper, Somerset County Museum, Taunton.

Mr. P. A. Stevens, Somerset County Museums Officer.

Mr. Nigel Collom, Taunton, Somerset.

Mr. Peter Preston, Manager, Wells Museum, Somerset.

Mr. David Chandler, Head of Department of War Studies and International Affairs, The Royal Military Academy, Sandhurst.

The Curator, Dorset County Museum, Dorchester, Dorset.

Mr. F. H. P. Barker, Curator, Warwick Castle, Warwick.

The owner of Holt Lodge Farm, Dorset.

Mr. Stephen Keen and his son, Monmouth Ash Farm, Dorset.

Philip Jackson and Mr. and Mrs. Geoffrey Taylor at the Holbrook House Hotel, Wincanton, for the abuse of their hospitality.

I am especially grateful to the photographer, Mr. Robert Chacksfield, who followed the campaign trail with me, and also the publisher, Mr. Rodney Legg, for his unfailing kindness and assistance in the preparation of this book.

K. Merle Chacksfield
Swanage, Dorset
May, 1985

Typeset by Timmy Taylor at TT Typesetting with contemporary photography
by Robert Chacksfield. Printed by Andrew Johnstone and Stephen Taylor at Wincanton Litho,
Old National School, North Street, Wincanton, Somerset.

International Standard book number [ISBN] 0 902129 70 8

James, Duke of Monmouth
From a portrait by Kneller
By courtesy of the National Portrait Gallery

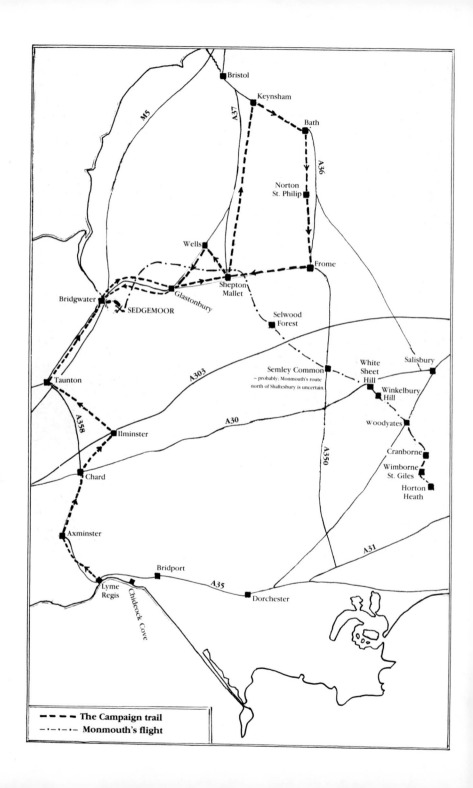

Bristol

Keynsham

Bath

A37

A36

M5

Norton
St. Philip

Wells

Frome

Shepton
Mallet

Glastonbury

Bridgwater

SEDGEMOOR

Selwood
Forest

White
Sheet
Hill

Salisbury

Taunton

A303

Semley Common
– probably; Monmouth's route
north of Shaftesbury is uncertain.

Winkelbury
Hill

A30

Woodyates

A358

Ilminster

A350

Cranborne

Chard

Wimborne
St. Giles

Horton
Heath

Axminster

A31

Bridport

A35

Lyme
Regis

Chideock Cove

Dorchester

- - - The Campaign trail

-·-·- Monmouth's flight

Contents

Lyme Regis from a print by J. Drayton Jnr., published by George Roberts in 'Life of James, Duke of Monmouth', 1844.

Setting the Scene

The events at Lyme Regis, the Dorset port which awoke to the beginning of the Western Rebellion on Thursday, 11th June 1685.
[Based on contemporary sources]

Early on the morning of Thursday, 11th June 1685, Mr. Samuel Dassell, Deputy Searcher of the Customs at the little Dorset port of **Lyme Regis** walked briskly down Broad Street to his office.

"Morning, Polly," he said, cheerily.

"Morning Mr. Dassell Sir."

"You are up betimes, and busy, I see."

"Yes sir. 'Tis best to get the work done before the day gets too hot," and Polly went on plying her broom.

"Morning Thomas," said the Deputy Searcher to Mr. Tye, the Surveyor of the Port of Lyme.

"Lovely day again," said Thomas Tye as he watched the sun rise across the bay, lighting the tops of the masts in the harbour.

"What do you make of those ships in the distance yonder, Sir?" went on Dassell. "I suppose they must be a league out to sea, and they're making slow progress."

Mr Tye took his glass and looked to the east of the bay into the rising sun. "Aye, Sam, I've been watching them. Strange somehow, they don't show their colours, and have made no signal nor fired a salute. Do you suppose they're coming in, or sailing on to the west?"

"It looks like there are three in all, and they don't look like smuggling vessels," said Dassell. "One of 'em is a frigate, but the other two smaller ones don't stand clear enough yet to see what they are."

"My, what a crowd is gathering hereabouts. 'Tisn't often we have such a press of people for a few ships coming up, unless they be smugglers or cargo vessels," said Tom, looking through his glass again. "I've got a strange feeling about those three," he went on. "Seems they've anchored off the shore there, and don't bestir themselves to make ready for landing passengers, nor do I see any move to prepare for unloading any cargo. Looks like they may be Dutch or French."

"I don't like it at all. I think it would be best to see what's afoot," urged Dassell.

"You're right, Sam. There's still no colours and no guns. I'm going out to board the frigate. Let's see, it's nearly ten now. I should be back in time to dine with you, and beat you at a game of bowls!"

With that, Mr Tye set out to board the Customs boat and pull across the bay to make some enquiries of the strange ships.

Meanwhile, the Mayor of Lyme, Captain Gregory Alford, a staunch Anglican Royalist merchant, had also noticed the little fleet making for the port. He rode down Broad Street and made his way across the cobbles towards Mr Samuel Dassell's office. Not a popular man, he received but few nods of recognition from the gathering groups of citizens gazing out to sea, despite the fact that he had but recently obtained a Charter for the town, and was the first Mayor elected to the new Borough. The celebrations on Charter day had finished with 'firing great guns and several volleys of small shot, and the night by making bonfires and all expressions of joy.' On arrival at the office, Captain Alford dismounted and blundered in.

"Well Dassell, good morning, good morning. What d'ye think of these vessels? Ye've seen them, I don't doubt. Can't make 'em out.

Where do they come from – d'ye know? Where's Tye? Shouldn't he be here?"

"Good morning Sir," replied Sam Dassell. "Indeed I've studied the ships, but I can't make them out either. One's a frigate, and there's a ketch of about a hundred tons, and another boat – I think they're all Dutch. No salute, no colours shown. Mr. Tye is suspicious, and he's pulling out now to board the frigate." "Good, good," replied the Mayor.

As they spoke, the Lyme Customs Officer – or 'Customer' as he was called – who lived along the coast at Chideock, burst in unceremoniously. "Your pardon, Sirs. I have news from **Chideock** for you," he said, breathlessly.

"Well, come on, come on, what is it?" demanded the Mayor. "You look spent, man. You must have come in haste. What's your news?"

"Well, sir, strange happenings in **Chideock Cove** prompted me to come to you. During my rounds early this morning I came upon some fishermen on the beach, and very merry they were. 'Ah!' thought I, 'so there's been some smuggled brandy or hollands landed, and it looks like they've been sampling the goods. Now I've got 'em!' I went over to them..."

"Well done!" said Sam. "We've been trying to nail that gang..."

"Wait a bit," said the Customer, "I've more to tell. When I got over to them they said, 'You've come too late.' 'How so?' I asked. 'Why, if you had come sooner you would have met with rich booty of contraband – canary and neats' tongues – and news of rebellion as well.'"

"Rebellion!" exclaimed the Mayor, with concern.

"Why, sir, that is what I said, and the fishermen told me they were seeing to their nets 'when out of the grey dawn came a ten-oared boat to the shore, and two gentlemen came over the side in affable and friendly mood and did talk with us. They had brought good canary wine and neats' tongues. We did enjoy this booty from the strangers, and they did laugh and eat and drink with us – gentlemen they were'..."

"Who were these gentlemen?" interrupted the Mayor. "Well, sir, I asked the men if there was anything more they could tell me. 'Yes,' they said. 'While we were drinking they asked 'What news?' 'We know of none,' say we, 'except a rebellion in Scotland.' 'Then,' said the visitors, 'we can give you news. There's another rebellion in Ireland, and it is believed that there will be one in England.' The fisherman said that they didn't like this, and had told them so. At this there came a signal from the frigate, and the boatmen rowed off back to their vessel, but the two gentlemen stayed on shore. They asked their way to Hawkchurch, and set off up the lane into the **Marshwood Vale**."

"So," said the Mayor, "did you find out the names of the gentlemen and where they came from?" "No," said the officer, "but one of the fishermen thought he heard something like 'Dare'."

"You have done well; you are to be commended." So saying, the Mayor, being considerably troubled by these events, and seeing that the ships were now slowly proceeding towards the harbour, decided to send two men to ride inland and warn the justices that two strangers from the shore at Chideock should be arrested and questioned. Having made these arrangements, and feeling very uneasy, he decided that he might as well continue with his normal Thursday activities with his friends, namely to have a meal, and then 're-create themselves at bowls' at the local bowling green on the Church Cliffs (since lost over Lyme's unstable lias cliffs, into the sea) which provided a fine view of the sea.

So they dined, and the Mayor, like Drake, then proceeded to play bowls that afternoon under the summer skies. Mr. Tye, however, did not appear for the meal, nor did he arrive for his promised game of bowls. His absence was not taken too seriously. It was suggested that perhaps 'the gaiety of their entertainment is responsible for detaining him,' or that the brisk off-shore wind meant that the ships had to come closer in to get him ashore.

Unlike Drake, the Mayor became increasingly disturbed during the day, and, having observed the vessels more closely, asked some seamen their opinion of them. They considered that they could be French, or Dutch, and it seemed unlikely that they were coming into Lyme, or they would have anchored further in the bay, closer to the Cobb, as the harbour wall is called. He constantly returned to the beach to monitor the ships. As the afternoon wore on he went to see if the 5 p.m. mail had arrived. It had, and the news it contained agitated the Mayor further, for it was reported from London: 'His Majesty had an account of three ships that had been laden with arms and double-manned from some port of Holland, entered there for the East Indies; but it was apprehended by His Majesty's Ambassador there that, whatever their pretences were, they would either land in England or Scotland, and that the Duke of Monmouth was aboard one of them.'

The Mayor, 'very uneasy,' together with Samuel Dassell and other companions, repaired to a tavern to discuss the situation. The loyal Dassell urged action: "The coming of these ships means ill, and the men aboard are doubtless rogues. I suggest that a great gun be fired, either to recall Mr. Tye, or, if they be friends, to invite them to answer with guns of civility and thanks."

17th century cannon on the harbour wall at Lyme Regis, pointing towards Golden Cap at Chideock.

Unfortunately there was no powder for the cannons mounted on shore, so no gun could be fired. The Mayor admitted shame-facedly that all the powder had been used at the recent celebrations of the Charter, and that he had not replenished the supply. "Then," said Dassell, "I'm damned if I know what's to be done."

They frequently left the tavern to see what the ships were doing. Towards evening they were horrified to see four boats, including Tye's, filled with men fully armed, within range of the shore, moving towards the west of the town. Lyme was utterly vulnerable. As the men rowed towards the Cobb the Mayor returned to the tavern and ordered the beating of the drums, whilst Dassell, being of a more practical turn of mind, dashed off to find some gunpowder. He came upon two merchants and said, "Sirs, you must have powder. There is a complaint for want of it."

"I have no powder ashore, Mr. Dassell," one replied, "but I have some in a vessel lately come from Barbados, now riding at anchor within the Cobb."

"Then, sir," said Dassell, "give me your orders to fetch the same on shore." The merchant agreed, and gave permission for four barrels. Dassell rowed out (in 1685 the Cobb was separated a little way from the shore, not joined to it as now) and reached the ship. At his request three barrels, which were none too large, were handed down to him.

"I have but four," explained the master, "and must keep one for our own defence, for my ship is my castle."

On deck, the seamen were firing off muskets without shot, to signal the alarm. By this time the invaders had reached the beach to the west of the Cobb, and as they were landing on the shingle Dassell remonstrated with the seamen on deck.

"It is better to load with shot your muskets and fire on those fellows that have just landed." "I cannot do so, for I know not if they be friends or enemies." "Be they what they will," retorted Dassell. "Let them be even the King's servants, none ought to presume in such a hostile manner to land without first giving notice to the Magistrate of their intent."

But the ship's master would not do so.

Dassell, accompanied by a lad from the ship, took the kegs of powder and, frustrated, pulled with all speed towards the Cobb gate. Keeping his eyes on the enemy landing on the west side, he thought that he saw well over a hundred men beginning to storm across the face of the cliff on the path leading to the town, but his estimate proved to be an exaggeration.

Among them was an athletic figure dressed in purple and wearing a star, armed only with a sword. As he stepped ashore, on the pebbles on the western side of the Cobb harbour, he knelt and gaves thanks to God for a safe voyage, and prayed for His blessing on the campaign. It was the Duke of Monmouth. Leaving the beach (known as "Monmouth's Beach" to this day) he drew his sword and, according to an old Devon fisherman who witnessed the scene, led his 82 men by the 'stile path' into the town, his banner of deep green showing the words, embroidered in gold, *"Fear nothing but God"*.

Dassell hurried into the town with his barrels of powder expecting to find the militia ready and waiting for it, but found only 'all things in

Monmouth Beach, Lyme Regis.

confusion,' and delivered the powder to two magistrates in Broad
Street. To his astonishment and despair he saw the Mayor fleeing with
all haste along the street and away from Lyme, urging his steaming
horse up the steep road leading to the west. He did not stop until, at
midnight, he reached **Honiton** in Devon, alerting the people as he
went. There he wrote a letter telling of the landing of Monmouth, with
an over-estimation of the number of men the Duke had brought with
him.

Samuel Dassell, with all speed, made his way home by way of Pound

Street. He saw men armed with muskets and pistols accompanied by shouting and cheering people and led by the Duke, smiling as his followers tried to kiss his hand. Ford, Lord Grey of Wark, walked by his side carrying a musket and pistol in his belt. They cheered his way, shouting excitedly, "*A Monmouth! A Monmouth! The Protestant Religion*". His standard was set up in a field at the east end of Lyme, and there his Declaration was read aloud to the people.

The Declaration, written by the Reverend Robert Ferguson, Chaplain to Monmouth's army, stated, amongst other things, 'That no Protestant of whatever persuasion soever, shall be molested or troubled for the exercise of this religion'. An annual election for Parliament would be held. Although the Duke had proof of his legitimacy, he would not immediately claim the throne, but would allow Parliament, freely elected, to determine the future Government of the country.

Dassell heard the Declaration as he stood in the crowd, and stayed in town long enough to satisfy himself that it was the Duke of Monmouth who had arrived in Lyme. He spoke to a man 'that looked of pleasant humour' and asked him what the invaders were doing in the town. "We come to fight the Papists," the man replied.

"Then," said Dassell, "your business is done, for here is none to fight you."

"Why, is not the Duke of York a Roman Catholic?"

"I know no such man, for he that was the Duke of York is now our Sovereign Lord the King." Dassell then asked where they were going, but was almost arrested by the man, so he decided, not unwisely, to remove himself from such attentions.

He later met Anthony Thorold, the Collector of Customs, and having seen the first recruits enlisted in Monmouth's army, they went home for some money, and on to the Mayor's house, where Captain Alford's daughter-in-law lent them a horse, and they 'rode double to the next stage which was **Crewkerne.**' Here they told their news, and wrote to the Duke of Albermarle at **Exeter**, and to Sir Edward Phelps and Colonel Luttrell at **Taunton**. Each now well horsed, they rode on to London and hurried to Sir Winston Churchill, the Member of Parliament for Lyme, who, accompanied by Brigadier Lord John Churchill, his son, brought them before the King at 4 a.m. on 13th June.

Having heard their story, the king permitted them to kiss his hand, and awarded them twenty pounds each. They repeated their information to the Privy Council and to Parliament at the Bar of the House.

The Rebellion had begun.

The Duke of Monmouth

The handsome Protestant Prince and the first conspiracy to kill his father and prevent his uncle, the Catholic Duke of York, from seizing the throne.

James Scott, Duke of Monmouth, was a tall young man with dark good looks and a friendly manner, who charmed all who met him. He was generally accepted to be the first-born illegitimate son of Charles II. Lucy Walters gave birth to him on 9th April, 1649, in Rotterdam, where she had been taken by her kinsman John Barlow. Charles II was then living in exile at the Hague, and Lucy became his mistress. It was the King himself who had his son christened James.

At the King's wish, James, when about nine years of age, was removed from the care of his mother and put in the charge of Lord Crofts, one of the King's friends, and he posed as a relative of his, and was known as James Crofts. The Queen Mother, Henrietta, had a great affection for him, and he lived for some time with her. At first he was brought up as a Roman Catholic, but then Charles thought it advisable that he should be instructed as a Protestant. Lucy Walters died in 1658.

In 1662, two years after the Restoration, the Queen Mother, at the King's request, brought James to Court. Charles provided for him, became very attached to the boy, and displayed his fondness publicly. He was a high spirited, amiable lad. Pepys described him in his diary on September 7th 1662 as 'Mr Crofts, the King's bastard, a most pretty spark of about fifteen years old.'

The first step towards James' advancement was the negotiation of his marriage to the 12-year-old daughter of the Countess of Wemys, Anne Scott, Countess of Buccleuch, a rich Scottish heiress. On 14 February 1663 he was created Baron of Tinedale, Earl of Doncaster and Duke of Monmouth, and later he was invested with the Order of the Garter. In the same year, at the age of fourteen, he was married to Anne Scott, and on 20 April he took the surname of Scott and was created Duke of Buccleuch.

The young nobleman showed a leaning towards military service, and in 1668 he was appointed Captain of His Majesty's Life Guards of Horse. During the Third Dutch war he served under his uncle, James Duke of York, with the fleet. He showed great bravery in battle, and received his uncle's commendation. He also acquitted himself well when commanding a brigade against the Dutch. "I owe my life to his bravery," Captain John Churchill said of Monmouth after the siege of Maastricht. Monmouth was interested in the welfare of his troops. He

14

improved their pay, and on his return from abroad he up-dated the Army drill along French lines.

He also distinguished himself against the rebel Scottish Covenanters at Bothwell Bridge, and even earned the respect of these Church of Scotland rebels for refusing to order his dragoons to pursue and massacre them when they fled. Charles complained of his leniency in this respect and told him, "If I had been there we would not have had the trouble of prisoners," to which his son replied: "I cannot kill men in cold blood. That's work only for butchers."

London received her favourite back with shouts of joy, and he was the hero of the hour.

When the succession to the throne became an urgent question, since Charles had no legitimate heir, Monmouth was taken up by Lord Shaftesbury and those others who wished to exclude the King's younger brother James, Duke of York because he was a Roman Catholic. The feeling of the public ran high. At one moment Monmouth was in banishment; at another he was hailed as the coming King.

Monmouth's 1680 tour of the West Country

In 1680 Monmouth set out on a quasi-royal tour of the West of England, where he was received with remarkable acclaim. Thomas Thynne welcomed him warmly at **Longleat**. He was equally well received by George Speke at **White Lackington**, and went on by way of **Forde Abbey, Hinton St George, Colyton** and **Otterton** to **Exeter**.

The ordinary people took him to their hearts. At Hinton St. George he touched Elizabeth Parcet for the King's Evil [Scrofula – growths in the lymph glands]. 'God bless your Greatness,' she said, and Monmouth answered, 'God bless you.' Within two days she was cured.

This augured well for Monmouth, as it confirmed to the people that he was of the Royal blood. As he went through Ilchester the people saw him as 'the hopes and head of the Protestant interest at that time, in opposition to the Duke of York and the Popish party, so that the affections of the people ran exceedingly after him.'

'We stood in the Friary Gate,' wrote John Whiting, a Quaker onlooker, 'as he rode through the town, and as he passed by, taking notice of so many Quakers together with their hats on, he stopped and put off his hat to us...we could not but have respect for his affability, and therefore were more concerned when his fall came.'

When he was about three miles from the city of Exeter he was greeted by between nine hundred and one thousand young men

Whitelackington and its chestnut tree, engraved for George Roberts who published the first 'Life of Monmouth'.

'clothed in linen waistcoats and drawers, white and harmless, having not so much as a stick in their hands.' When the Duke met them, he 'rid up first between them and then around each company; after which they united, and went hand in hand, in order before the Duke, into the city, where he was no sooner arrived but a universal shout from all parts echoed forth his welcome.'

He was welcomed again at Longleat, and from there he returned to London 'wonderfully pleased with the noble and generous entertainment he had met with at the several places where he came, every place striving to outvie each other.'

The people were delighted to see Monmouth, as they had never had the happiness to see His Majesty or any member of the royal family before. His popularity alarmed, in particular, his uncle James, Duke of York. Monmouth made another tour to the West Country in September 1682.

His father's affection for him declined after the upheaval of the "*Rye House Plot*" in 1683. This was a plan conceived by a few desperate men to assassinate both the King and the Duke of York – in order to secure Monmouth's succession – but it was soon discovered and

16

foiled. Monmouth had had no part in it, and indeed would have recoiled with horror from the thought of parricide, but the indignation aroused in the country extended to include the whole Whig faction. The Earl of Essex was found dead in the Tower of London with his throat slit, and Lord William Russell and Algernon Sidney were executed there. Monmouth was associated with prominent Whigs such as Lord Shaftesbury, who fled to Holland and died there in 1683.

Monmouth threw himself on his father's mercy, and was forgiven, but he soon gave further offence, and thought it prudent to go into voluntary exile. He quitted the country and found refuge in Holland, where he was living when, in 1685, Charles II died, and James, Duke of York, became King James II.

The Earl of Argyll, one of Scotland's leading noblemen, was in Holland actively planning an expedition to Scotland to raise rebellion against the new king, and Monmouth was persuaded to consider leading a similar expedition to land in the West of England. He sent Christopher Battiscombe, a young lawyer and Dorset landowner from **Bettiscombe Manor**, with urgent messages to John Trenchard of **Taunton** and others of his friends in the West Country warning them to be prepared for a landing 'against the beginning of May.'

On 10th April, 1685, King James' Special Envoy at the Hague, Bevil Skelton, arrived to warn the Dutch authorities of the exiles who had taken refuge in their country, and to try to persuade them to banish them, and so prevent them from raising a rebellion in England. In May Skelton sent information to the Earl of Middleton saying 'it is whispered about that Monmouth intends speedily to pass over into England and land in the west part of that Kingdom, and that Mathews and those who are gone before are sent to prepare for his reception.' Edward Mathews was one of Monmouth's supporters, and was to be Lieutenant Colonel of the Yellow Regiment of the Duke's army. Skelton later reported that Monmouth had 'disappeared'. Fresh information revealed that Monmouth had not sailed for Scotland with Argyll, as was at first thought, but that he was busy raising men and chartering ships for a rising in England.

Meanwhile, Argyll had landed in Scotland. Orders were sent to Deputy Lieutenants and Mayors of towns, especially in the West Country, to disarm all dangerous and suspected persons.

Desperate for money with which to buy arms, Monmouth sold his jewellery and that of his mistress, Henrietta Wentworth. Nothing was forthcoming from England, but friends in Holland contributed about £3,000, and Le Blon, a Dutch merchant, helped to provide him with the shipping he needed. He acquired four small cannon, 1500 muskets and pikes, and a similar quantity of breastplates. Despite attempts by Skelton to prevent the expedition from sailing, Monmouth embarked at Santford on 24th May, but was unable at first, owing to unfavourable winds, to reach his 32 gun frigate *Helderenberg*, waiting in the Texel, but after some delay, as Captain Tellier, who was in a dogger, one of the two smaller ships, later reported, Monmouth 'in great secrecy, and disguised in seamen's apparel and with great whiskers' had reached the frigate.

Further evidence of Monmouth's venture was discovered by King James when on 30th May a letter to a James Carrier, blacksmith, was intercepted, and from this it was deduced that **Taunton** might be the meeting place of the rebel sympathisers, but since the King did not know where Monmouth would land, his army remained in London.

So Monmouth sailed, and the rebellion was under way. Evading the naval vessels which were cruising the Channel looking for him, his little fleet, beating against a westerly gale, took ten days to reach their destination. The choice of landing was **Lyme Regis**, and it was in Lyme Bay on 11th June 1685, that the three ships arrived, to give Mayor Alford and Samuel Dassell such concern.

The Old George Inn, Lyme Regis. It was burnt down on May 11th, 1844, as George Roberts was printing his 'Life of Monmouth' in which it appears. Monmouth made his headquarters here whilst he was in Lyme Regis.

The Campaign in the West

*The Monmouth Rebellion of 1685 galvanised the general
population of the western counties — but the rebel force
was a peasant army, and from the start its leaders
showed their failings too.*

Thursday, 11th June and Friday, the 12th.

As the news of Monmouth's landing spread rapidly throughout the
West Country, hundreds came to enlist under his flag. Almost
immediately sixty keen young men joined, were armed by daybreak,
and sent to join the officers who guarded the approaches to the town
of Lyme Regis. The vigorous young Protestant Champion took an
active interest in the men, welcoming them to his forces. He said to
one of the first volunteers as he seized his arm: "Sir, thou art an honest
fellow, and I'll take care and provide for thee; thou deservest
encouragement. I have arms enough for thee and many more; be they
twenty or thirty thousand, I've arms enough for all!"

The rebel army, of which Lord Grey was second in command,
assisted by Andrew, Lord Fletcher of Saltoun and Captain Jones,
continued to gather forces, and Ferguson, the Duke's Chaplain,
recorded the names of the recruits. As the cool evening shadows
lengthened, and throughout the night, men tumbled from their homes
and rushed down the cobbled streets; farm labourers, blacksmiths,
carpenters, weavers, all eager to back the Cause. Monmouth made his
headquarters at the George Inn in Coombe Street, then the principal
hostelry in **Lyme Regis**. (It burnt down in 1844) Hundreds of men
were coming into the town, but it was noticeable that men of land and
substance were not among them. Many of Monmouth's friends had
been arrested on suspicion, and the gentry held aloof. There were no
risings in London.

As the Duke's force increased they were drilled as quickly as
possible in the use of arms under the veterans from the Cromwellian
forces. Regiments were being formed as had been planned during the
voyage to Lyme. First was the Duke's own Regiment, the Red
Regiment, under Lieutenant Colonel Thomas Venner, with Major
Nathaniel Wade, a cool, competent lawyer from Bristol. Thomas Dare,
one of the two mysterious 'gentlemen' who had entertained the
fishermen on the beach at **Chideock**, (now called **Seatown** beach)
before the main landing, and who had left from there for **Forde Abbey**,
was to be Paymaster.

The White Regiment was formed under Lieutenant Colonel John Foulkes, with senior officers Major Manley and Captain Francis Goodenough. Lieutenant Colonel Abraham Holmes commanded the Green Regiment, with Major Robert Parsons and Captain Palchall. Some men of this Regiment were recuited from London. The fourth Regiment, the Blue Regiment, with recruits from Taunton and Wellington, was led by Lieutenant Colonel Richard Bovet.

The Artillery, whose armament consisted of the four small cannon, was under the command of Anton Buyse, 'the Brandenberger', an experienced gunner from Holland. The Surgeon was a Cornishman of twenty-six years who had been studying at Leyden University, and the Army Chaplain was the Reverend Robert Ferguson, whilst the Duke had his own Domestic Chaplain, the Reverend Nathaniel Hook. One John Kidd, an experienced militiaman, who was in Holland to buy horses for the Earl of Devonshire at the time when the expedition was about to depart, was offered a captaincy in the army, and there was also an Independent Company from Lyme Regis of eighty soldiers.

In Lyme the Duke divided his men into three companies, two being appointed to guard 'the avenues of the town,' whilst the remaining third was to unload the arms and the ammunition from the three ships. Major Wade's task was to land the four pieces of cannon and see that

The Old Monmouth Hotel, Church Street, Lyme Regis, reputed to have been the billet for Monmouth's Cavalry under Lord Grey.

they were mounted. This he managed to do by daybreak, ably assisted by mariners and townsmen. However, the major part of the arms and ammunition was never brought to shore, for some days later the man o' war *Saudadoes*, under Captain Trevenion, captured the two smaller vessels, the pink, a flat-bottomed craft from the shallow Dutch inshore waters, and the dogger, a two-masted Dutch North Sea fishing smack, and the Captain reported that he took forty barrels of powder and stocks of 'backs, breasts and potts' enough for four or five thousand men.

So Monmouth was now hard pressed for ammunition, and he also lacked horses. He scoured the coutryside for them, and being also short of money, he 'borrowed' £400 from the Customs House, leaving a receipt to be honoured later. He also took the borough's new Charter.

In Dalrymple's Memoirs it is stated that 'at first the Duke was in straits for provisions, but Ferguson, having assured him that he would find subsistence for one day for the army if the Duke would give him command of it for a minute, and the Duke having consented, Ferguson gave orders that the soldiers should observe the next day as a solemn fast for success.'

Saturday, 13th June.

Early in the morning Thomas Dare returned from Forde Abbey, Somerset, with a party of forty horses and men, some well armed, and he himself riding the best of the horses. Fletcher, a fiery Scottish laird, was reckoned to be the finest cavalry officer in the army. After dining with Monmouth and Lord Grey, Fletcher assumed an officer's prerogative and mounted Dare's horse, and there ensued a fierce quarrel between the two men, which ended when Fletcher shot Dare in the head and killed him. Dare's son, who was present, protested violently at his father's murder, and Monmouth ordered Fletcher to return to the *Helderenburg* frigate. The loss of these two very able men was a tragedy for the Duke which probably affected the whole of the subsequent campaign. As Dalrymple said, 'with Fletcher all chance of success in war left Monmouth.' His best officer was gone, and from now on his destiny lay in the hands of his worst, Lord Grey.

Having lost Thomas Dare, Monmouth appointed Captain Goodenough from the White Regiment to be Paymaster in his own Regiment. Dare had been a man of much wealth, and great influence for the Cause in **Taunton**, and the events threw gloom over Monmouth and his followers, but he continued with his preparations, and planned a night attack on the Dorset Militia at **Bridport**. Lord Grey was in command of the venture, with Colonel Venner to advise him, and he had some forty horse and four hundred foot, the latter under Wade and Goodenough. The rebel army set off across the little hills of west Dorset to **Chideock** and **Allington**, a hamlet adjoining the western side of Bridport. They covered the distance of ten miles during the night and reached the bridge at Allington.

Wade recorded later that substantial numbers of horses, about forty or fifty, were gathered in from the neighbourhood, and news came that there were people in Bridport who were ready to join the rebels if the Constable's Guard of the town could be kept out of the way. Major Manley rode off with fifteen horses mounted 'for the most part by officers and gentlemen who came over with the Duke, to bring off the persons willing to join them, but they found not only the Constable's watch but a troop of Militia Horse to oppose them, which the Major charged and routed, killing two of the troopers; but finding them supported by a greater force, retreated to Lyme without pursuit, or a man wounded.'

At the end of the day Monmouth's forces amounted to a thousand foot and one hundred and fifty horse. Rumours that the Duke of Albemarle was approaching ready to attack caused him to march out a force of eight hundred foot and a hundred and fifty horse with three pieces of cannon, and they lay in wait in hedges and along the narrow roads. The foot soldiers lay in the fields with their arms, and the horsemen stood holding their bridles in their hands. The rumours, however, proved false, and no attack materialised.

Sunday, 14th June.

Early on Sunday morning a thick mist covered the town of **Bridport**. Grey had been informed that there were strong forces of twelve hundred foot and a hundred horse defending the town, but as he came out of the mist he found the bridge thinly guarded, and what guards there were retreated to rejoin the Militia encamped in a field beyond the bridge. Colonel Venner, second in command of Monmouth's Regiment, swept into the town, to find only riderless horses running about the street, and he sent a request to Lord Grey to support him with his cavalry.

During the advance firing broke out from the windows of the **Bull Inn**, where some officers of the Militia were based. The inn was promptly attacked, the doors were broken open, and several lives were lost. In the exchange of fire Venner killed two Dorset gentlemen, Edward Coker and Wadham Strangways, and other officers were wounded. In the Parish Church in Bridport is a brass plaque on the wall

The Bull Hotel, Bridport, where some officers of the Dorset Militia were based on the 14th June, 1685, and which saw the first skirmish of Monmouth's campaign.

of St. Catherine's Chapel, a part of the Church now used as a vestry. It reads:

> 'In memory of Edward Coker, Gent., second son of Captain Robert Coker of Mapowder, slain at the Bull Inn, in Bridport, June 14, A.D. 1685, by one Vener, who was an officer under the later Duke of Monmouth, in that rebellion.'

Two managed to escape by hiding in an attic, and 'in a plot of kidney beans'. Then Colonel Venner himself was 'much dismayed' by being shot in the stomach, and gave the order to retreat. Lord Grey's horses bolted at the sound of gunfire, and as Wade later reported, 'The flight of Lord Grey so discouraged the vanguard of the foot that they threw down their arms and began to run, but I bringing up another body to their succour, they were persuaded to take up arms again.' Wade guarded the bridge, expecting the Militia to attack, but they remained out of musket range, and each side merely shouted abuse at the other.

The rebels then 'retreated in pretty good order with twelve or fourteen prisoners and about thirty horses'. Near **Charmouth** they met Monmouth coming to their aid. Somewhat suprised to find them marching in good order, he asked whether it was true that Lord Grey had run away. Wade confirmed this, and later expressed his surprise that the Duke permitted Lord Grey to retain his command in spite of his behaviour.

There is no doubt that Monmouth was considerably concerned about the state of his cavalry, and would not have much faith in it for the rest of the campaign. Wade was advanced to the rank of Colonel and appointed to the command of the Regiment now that Venner was wounded.

After a short respite the Duke informed Colonel Wade that he must be prepared to march early the next morning. He had information that the Duke of Albermarle with the Devonshire men, and the Duke of Somerset and his men were, approaching to contain the army. As it was, he left it almost too late.

Monday, 15th June.

At about 10 a.m. Monmouth marched out of **Lyme Regis**, never to return. Colonel Wade noted that whilst he had been at Bridport the force had increased in numbers, and the Duke moved inland to **Axminster** 'at the head of three thousand men who wore green boughs in their hats and cheered for Monmouth and the Protestant religion.'

The Duke probably went over the high ground by **Hunter's Lodge Inn**, and his scouts must have gone as far as **Trinity Hill** [*Shute Hill*], which gave a fine view of the Axe valley, to observe the Devonshire Militia on the one side and the Somerset Militia on the other hastening to join forces at Axminster. The scouts of the Somerset Militia had already entered the town, but on the approach of Monmouth's troops, who had doubled their pace, they fled, and the rebel army occupied Axminster.

Monmouth guarded the town with cannon and musketeers. He posted Colonel Wade with his Regiment, supported by the 'Brandenburger' Buyse and his artillery, to watch the approach of the Devonshire forces, and Wade dispersed his men along the hedges lining the approach roads. As the men of Devon came near, they saw what they thought to be cannon threatening them from the hedges.

These, in fact, were not Buyse's artillery, but well-placed tree trunks, but the Devonshires, without waiting to find out, turned and ran. Wade started after them, but Monmouth held him back, saying 'his business was not to fight but to march on.' The Somerset forces, shouting that they had been betrayed, were also routed, many of them abandoning coats and arms under the hedges, which were found and brought to the rebels. The Axminster Dissenters wrote in their book, 'The Lord eminently appeared, sending an Hornett of fear amongst those that came to oppose them.'

John Coad, a member of the Somerset Militia, had been sickened by the 'hellish oaths and ribaldry' of his comrades, and splashed across the Axe to join Monmouth's army. He was impressed by the warm welcome he received, and by the ban on swearing, thieving and plundering.

Albermarle drew off his forces towards **Honiton** and the Somerset Militia withdrew to the east. Opposition to Monmouth had been limited to these unsuccessful forays by the local Militia, but sterner force was beginning to move against him.

John, Lord Churchill, who in 1704 would become the nation's hero for defeating the French and Bavarians at Blenheim, had ridden west with some four hundred troopers, hardened fighting men, and the brutal Colonel Percy Kirke was also on the way with five hundred experienced infantrymen – ironically known as *Kirke's Lambs* from the shoulder flashes they wore – whilst moving more slowly were five companies under Churchill's younger brother Charles, who were escorting the artillery from Portsmouth.

Reproduction of Lamb & Flag badge now in the Somerset County Museum, probably as worn by 'Kirke's Lambs'. *Photograph by courtesy of the Somerset County Museum.*

Lord Churchill had arrived in the vicinity of Axminster before the main body of his troops, and was dismayed by the feeble showing of the Militia. He wrote to the King: 'Unless speedy course be taken we are like to lose this country to the rebels; for we have two regiments run away a second time...and there is not any relying on those regiments that are left unless we had some of your Majesty's standing forces to lead them on and encourage them.' If Monmouth could have attacked speedily at this time, or even on later occasions, his rebellion could probably have become a successful revolution, but throughout his campaign he failed to take advantage of the situation by quick decisive action.

Tuesday, 16th June.

Colonel Wade having camped outside Axminster near **Membury Down** above Chard, the rebel army marched unhindered to **Chard**, where they camped in a field near the town. Monmouth was greatly upset by the failure of the Whig gentry to come to his aid, and especially by the lack of support by the men of the *"Green Ribbon Club"* who had promised to help the Protestant Duke during his early progress through the West. However, they were joined here by John Speke, son of the 'old Gentleman' George Speke of **Whitelackington**, who had himself prudently absconded at the outset of the rebellion. John Speke brought with him 'a company of ragged horse' and some 'ordinary fellows,' and was made a colonel of the army. Seeking arms and horses, a party went back to **Forde Abbey**, but they had little success. They discovered that Mr. Edmund Prideaux, the owner, had been taken away by a King's Messenger, and all that they could lay hands on were some coach horses, which were taken under protest from Mrs. Prideaux.

It was at Chard that Ferguson first proposed that the Duke of Monmouth be proclaimed King. This was supported by Lord Grey, but some, including Wade, were against it. The Duke's army was here joined by one hundred and fifty six recruits.

Wednesday, 17th June.

The Duke progressed to **Ilminster**, and encamped at **Winterhay**, about half a mile beyond the town. He was now closely followed by Lord Churchill, who was hoping for reinforcements, but although the Wiltshire Militia has been mustered at the Market Place in **Salisbury**, and other Militia troops of horse were sent to the New Forest, he did not yet move against Monmouth.

At Ilminster Square, Monmouth met Charles Speke, a relation of John

Speke, who came to him and shook his hand. In consequence of that friendly gesture, Charles Speke was later hanged by Judge Jeffreys. More recruits from **Axminster** were welcomed to the swelling ranks of the rebel army.

King James ordered Monmouth's Declaration to be burnt, and a bill of attainder for treason was rushed through Parliament, whilst five thousand pounds was put upon Monmouth's head, dead or alive. Lord Sunderland, Secretary of State, wrote to Brigadier Churchill informing him of the appointment of Louis de Duras, the Earl of Feversham, as Commander-in-Chief of the Royal army, with himself, Churchill, as Second-in-Command, and further appointments were announced as more units were grouped for battle. Some of the Somerset Militia who had retreated from Axminster were in **Taunton** when news reached them that Monmouth was advancing on that town, and at midnight they fled, abandoning ammunition. Their officers ordered them to appear at **Bridgwater** the next day, but none of them did so, and neither did their officers.

At about 4 p.m. the advance cavalry of the rebel army, led by Captain Hucker, a rich merchant of Taunton, entered that town, and freed some prisoners. The warm, dry weather had favoured the rebels, and they were able to camp and march under good conditions.

Thursday, 18th June.

Moving on from **Ilminster**, the main body of the army marched through **Hatch Green**, **Stoke St Mary** and **Shoreditch** and encamped in a field at the west end of **Taunton**. Rumours were rife that James II had died, and all who had a horse or could borrow one rode out to meet the Duke, who might become their new King. The narrow streets of the town were thronged with people and strewn with flowers. Here was a town where the majority of the people were Protestant Dissenters, and they vied with each other in showing their affection for the Duke, whilst the businessmen opened their houses to him and his followers and gave them food, drink and supplies of every kind.

The Duke issued a stern order, read to the men in camp by Captain Goodenough the Paymaster, warning them against an excess of zeal in getting horses and goods, and robbing and pillaging the good people of all they had. He commanded 'that from henceforth they presume not to seize or take any horse from any person whatever, commanding the same on pain of death to everyone that shall offend therein.'

Captain Hucker gave Monmouth hospitality at his house, which is reputed to have been near the **Three Cups Inn**, where the **County Hotel** is now, and he made his headquarters there.

Friday, 19th June.

The crowds of men who were rallying to the banner were still in a frenzy of excitement, and shouts for Monmouth's cause arose from the crowds, '*A Monmouth! A Monmouth!*' The young leader had his way strewn with flowers; the windows, decorated with green boughs, were thronged with spectators, and hats were sprigged. He was received with such joy and acclamation that 'one would have thought the people's wits were flown away in the flights of their joy.' The magistrates who remained in the town were forced to attend the Market Square to hear the Declaration.

The memorable ceremony of the Procession of the '*Maids of Taunton*' took place, a parade of girls from the seminaries of Miss Blake and Mrs. Musgrave who, one story goes, had torn open twenty-seven of their silk petticoats to make colours for the Duke of Monmouth, one embroidered with 'a Golden Flag, J. R., a crown fringed with lace.' These girls were from well-to-do families in Taunton. The charming procession, led by Miss Blake with 'a naked sword in one hand and a small, curious Bible in the other,' went down the street to Captain Hucker's house and called for the Duke of Monmouth.

The Duke came out with Lord Grey and both 'saluted each girl.' The leader, Miss Blake, introduced by Captain Bovet, made a little speech and presented the Duke with the Bible, at which he, 'in a manner transported,' assured her that he came 'to defend the truths contained in that book and to seal it with his blood if there should be occasion for it.' His Grace mounted his horse, and the twenty-seven young ladies followed, each bearing a coloured banner and attended by an armed trooper, down the street to the ringing of the church bells and the cheers of the crowds.

During the Duke's arrival at Taunton, Lord Churchill and six troops of dragoons were on the move in the West Country. Some of Churchill's men on patrol had moved out of Chard towards **Ilminster** and **Taunton**, and had come upon a small party of Monmouth's outposts in the forest of **Ashill**. There a skirmish took place, at **Fight Ground**, in which four rebels were killed, including Lieutenant Moreaux, one of Lord Oxford's Regiment. Churchill's men returned to **Chard** after the group of rebels was dispersed. Wade said, 'During out stay here we had slain Cornett Legg, in a horse skirmish near the town.'

Saturday, 20th June.

Having finally been persuaded by Lord Grey and Ferguson, and probably overwhelmed by the enthusiasm and adulation of the people, Monmouth was, at the **Market Cross** in **Taunton**, proclaimed King in the presence of the people, and of some magistrates dressed in their robes, who had been forced to attend. The New Declaration, read by a man named Tilley from Bristol stated that 'Upon the decease of our Sovereign Lord Charles the Second, the right of succession to the Crown of England, Scotland, France and Ireland with the Dominions and Territories thereunto belonging, did legally descend and devolve upon the most illustrious and high born Prince James, Duke of Monmouth, son and heir-apparent to the said King Charles the Second.' Other proclamations were read against King James and the royal army, and it was ordered that the posts should pass freely, and that anyone collecting taxes in James's name should be branded 'rebel and traitor.'

The townsmen of Taunton were 'brisk boys,' and constituted some of the best of Monmouth's troops. The continuing scarcity of arms, however, troubled him considerably, and he decided to form a body of 'scythe-men' to act as grenadiers. The scythes were to be firmly fixed at the end of straight, stout handles, and made formidable weapons. A warrant was sent out by *James R* – the 'new' King's style was identical with that of the 'real' King – to constables and tything men in the area 'to search for, seize, and take all scythes as can be found in your tything, paying a reasonable price for the same, and bring them to my house tomorrow by one of the clock in the afternoon, that they may be delivered to the commission officers that are appointed to receive them at Taunton by four of the same day, and you shall be re-imbursed by me what the scythes are worth...Given under my hand this 20th day of June in the first year of His Majesty's reign. To the Tything Men of Ch.' [*Chedzoy?*] The company of the scythemen was attached to Monmouth's Red Regiment together with one hundred and sixty horse, commanded by Captain John Hucker and Captain Tucker.

Learning that Albermarle was at Wellington, the Duke made some small entrenchments on the roads leading in that direction and sent out strong guards under Wade's command to man these defences. Wade was there all night, and when discharged from duty on the 20th he said, 'This was the first night we lay in beds after our coming over.'

The new 'King' called a council of war at Taunton. He always hoped that John Churchill and other friends with whom he had shared previous campaigns would not now oppose him, but he did not allow this hope to influence his plans. They discussed whether they should return to fight Albermarle, or whether to march on, and finally decided to go on to **Bridgwater** and **Bristol**, which at this time was the largest provincial city in England. Because there were now two King Jameses in Somerset, the Duke was called 'King Monmouth' – a designation that has survived in western folk memory for 300 years.

Sunday, 21st June.

The weather, which had been so favourable, began to deteriorate as they marched towards **Bridgwater**. The Duke of Somerset now informed Whitehall of Monmouth's movements, and Feversham ordered him to leave four companies in **Bath** and march to **Bristol**. The Duke of Beaufort had orders to break down the bridge over the Avon at **Keynsham.** 'The King thinks much of the importance of Bristol' said Beaufort's orders, and the King also thought it wise to have two ships to 'apprehend vessels coming into the Severn.'

Monmouth was again received with great enthusiasm at Bridgwater, where he was greeted by the Mayor, Mr Alexander Popham, and members of the Corporation, who carried him to **High Cross** and proclaimed him King. He was then taken to his lodgings at **Bridgwater Castle**, whilst his men encamped in Castle Field. He now had a Lifeguard of forty young men, 'well mounted and armed, and paying their own expenses.' Oldmixon reported that the cavalry now amounted to one thousand horses; 'mares, geldings and colts.' He also had six thousand foot in six regiments. 'We had very good quarters at Bridgwater,' said Wade, 'and for the most part free.'

John Churchill went to church at **Chard**, where the text was from Romans 13: 'And they that resist shall receive to themselves damnation.' Monmouth had denied the voluble Reverend Ferguson the opportunity of preaching in the fine church of **St Mary Magdalen** at **Taunton** because of their early departure, but Ferguson could not be restrained from preaching to the army on its way to Bridgwater. His text was from Deuteronomy 20: 'Hear, O Israel, ye approach the day into battle against your enemies. Let not your hearts faint, fear not, and do not tremble, neither be terrified because of them; for the Lord your God is he that goeth with you, to fight for you against your enemies, to save you.'

But it rained.

Monday, 22nd June.

Instead of remaining in **Bridgwater** to train his raw recruits as he intended, Monmouth, probably nervous because of Churchill's attacks on his outposts, moved out of the town and pressed eastwards towards **Glastonbury** and **Wells** instead of taking the more direct route by **Axbridge** to Bristol. The rain poured in torrents, drenching the men and making it doubly difficult for them and their horses as they dragged themselves through the flooded lanes and the mud, with the four little cannon pulled by oxen and horses. Only two regiments reached Wells, the rest taking shelter in the town of Glastonbury, or in the **Abbot's**

The Abbot's Kitchen, Glastonbury Abbey, where some of Monmouth's men rested and dried out on 22nd June, 1685.

Kitchen nearby, or in the ruins of **Glastonbury Abbey**, which were more extensive then than they are today. Monmouth himself seems likely to have camped here, for a proclamation is dated 'our camp at Glastonbury, June 23rd.'

The men lit large fires amongst the ruins to try to dry themselves out. They had plenty of provision from the townspeople. Wade reported: 'In our march this day we were alarmed by a troop of my Lord of Oxford's Horse, and on the other side had news that the Militia had left Wells and were retreated to Bath and Bristol.' It was whilst they were at Glastonbury that a member of the Bridgwater Clubmen, a force formed during the Civil War to protect their part of the country from raiding armies, came to Monmouth and assured him of their support. In this belief he enrolled the 'Club Army' under his banner, but instead of the promised several thousand reinforcements, only a few – one hundred and sixty – actually appeared by the end of the rebellion.

Tuesday, 23rd June.

Monmouth and his imposing force left **Glastonbury** for **Shepton Mallet**. Churchill put pressure on the rebel forces by continual harassment on their journey towards **Bristol**, and his close presence prevented further searches for supplies by the rebel patrols. Once in Shepton Mallet they were again welcomed, and men were quartered in houses and sheltered from the rain. Edward Strode of **Downside**, a mile and a half on the old road from Bath, presented to Monmouth a gift of one hundred guineas, and a carrier, Bernard Wilkins, supplied the rebel forces with grain for their horses and provisions, saying that he would not take a farthing for his goods until they had won.

During this part of the campaign it was said that 'the rank and file had been given to understand they were marching for London, where they expected to arrive on June the 27th, and place King Monmouth on the throne.' At Shepton Mallet another Council of War was set up. The Duke told Wade of his intention to attack Bristol on the Somerset side. Wade, a Bristol man, advised him to 'pass over the Avon at Keynsham Bridge, and attack it on the Gloucestershire side.' Monmouth agreed, and decided to take his advice.

Wednesday, 24th June.

The army turned north and marched for **Keynsham**. Unknown to Monmouth, Feversham had already entered **Bristol**, and hearing that the rebels were at **Shepton Mallet**, had made plans to intercept them. In the poor weather the troops were making slow progress, but they finally reached **Pensford**. Wade said, 'We were all this day alarmed in the rear by a party of Horse and Dragoons. Nevertheless we lodged quietly that night in Pensford within five miles of Bristol, where we met with nothing remarkable but that we perceived a great fire in or near Bristol that night by the redness of the sky. We had supposed that they had set the suburbs on fire lest we should have possessed ourselves of it, but it seems it was accidentally set on fire.'

It was, in fact, a burning ship, the *Abraham and Mary*, by the quay – an attempt, some say, to create confusion.

Keynsham Bridge today; the original was washed away.

The continual harassment by the Royal troops as the rebels approached the city, together with the lack of fervent support from the inhabitants, was depressing to Monmouth. His looks were despondent. Later that night, on receiving news that the bridge at Keynsham had been demolished, the Duke sent 'a troop of Horse under the command of Captain Tily to possess the town and repair the bridge.' It was repaired by daybreak, and Tily also scattered a troop of Gloucestershire Militia, who left behind two horses and a prisoner.

Thursday, 25th June.

At about ten o'clock in the morning Monmouth marched his forces safely across the bridge, intending to attack **Bristol** that night, using as guides local men from the city who were in his forces, but the weather was so bad that he postponed the attack and took his whole army back to **Keynsham** village for the night. This village, lying south of the road between Bath and Bristol, was a wide open area well able to provide ample room for the troops. The army had hardly taken up their quarters before they were attacked by two troops of cavalry, thirty horse under Captain Parker, and Lieutenant Colonel Theophilus Oglethorpe with twenty-five guards, 'with whom our Horse unadvisedly engaged.' Fourteen or fifteen rebels were killed, amongst whom was Brand, Captain of Horse.

The royalists left behind three prisoners, who told the Duke that Feversham and about four thousand of the King's army were close at hand outside **Bristol**. He had also heard that the Duke of Beaufort would burn the city if the gates were opened to Monmouth, at which he is reported to have said: 'God forbid that I should be accessary to the ruin of my friends, or that for any consideration I should subject so great a city to the double calamity of sword and fire.'

The news of the proximity of Feversham's army forced Monmouth to change his mind about attacking Bristol. With his officers he debated whether to proceed to Gloucester, and on to Shropshire and Cheshire, where he had loyal supporters, or to march into Wiltshire. The arguments were 'that it was four days' march to Gloucester,' that 'our soldiers want shoes,' and that there was a considerable body of dragoons who would harry them. Despondently, they decided to make for **Bath** that very night. Feversham and his horse made their way along the north side of the river Avon to Bath also.

Friday, 26th June.

Reaching the hills above Bath in the early morning, a trumpeter was sent by Monmouth to order the surrender of the city and to summon the garrison to join him, but, as Wade said, 'Only in Bravado, for we had no expectation of its surrender.' The trumpeter was shot dead by the sentries. After this the army marched south to **Norton St. Philip**, where the Duke made his headquarters at the **Old House**, now the **George Inn**, and posted his four cannon outside the door by the market cross. The foot were nearby in the fields with their officers, and the cavalry were in the town. The construction of some defences was begun whilst Monmouth reviewed his plans.

Wade said, 'Here the Duke was very disconsolate and began to complain that all the people had deserted him, for there was no

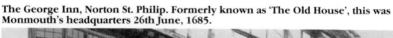

The George Inn, Norton St. Philip. Formerly known as 'The Old House', this was Monmouth's headquarters 26th June, 1685.

appearance of the Wiltshire Horse Mr. Adlam talked of, although we were near enough to have joined them if they had had any stomach to it. Indeed, the Duke was so dejected that we could hardly get orders from him.'

It must have finally dawned on the Duke that he would, after all, have to fight an army which he had previously known and commanded in battle for something like seventeen years. The rebel army was in a bad way. There had been several alarms during the night, but no serious developments. News came that the people of **Frome** had proclaimed him King, but later messages said that Pembroke and his Militia had entered the town and torn down the rebel placards.

And it rained!

Saturday, 27th June.

Monmouth's intention was to move out along the road another five miles to **Frome** to find shelter for his men, for the rain was continuous. There he would review his plans for the next move. Just as the rebels were striking camp they were attacked. The Duke of Grafton and Colonel Kirke with five hundred musketeers, followed by infantry, cannon and horses, had arrived on the outskirts of **Norton St. Philip**, and a battle developed.

As usual, the Duke of Monmouth had left the approaches well guarded. Under Captain Vincent and fifty musketeers he had had a barricade erected across a lane which was on each side lined with good thick hedges. 'Just by this barricade was a little byway which led into the back part of the town through a Gentleman's court near to where the foot were encamped in two fields.' In continuous rain Monmouth's rebels fought well, and there was much hand-to-hand fighting. By going through the 'Gentleman's court' they were able to engage the Royalists on three sides, 'save the left flank by which through the hedge many of them escaped.'

The Duke of Grafton had his horse shot from under him, and avoided being taken prisoner only by leaping on to a wounded horse. Feversham lost many men in the fierce hand-to-hand fighting.

Monmouth lacked the cavalry with which to finish the matter with a good charge, but bringing up the foot and lining the hedge with them, with the cavalry behind, he positioned 'two pieces of cannon into the mouth of the lane and guarded them with a company of Sithmen,' and the remaining two on an eminence on the right side of the lane, and so consolidated the position.

Both sides began to cannonade each other, and kept it up in pouring rain for six hours. Finally Colonel Venner, who had recovered from the wound he received at Bridport, advised the Duke to retreat – but he determined to stand firm and continue with the battle, and it was Feversham who decided to retreat. Monmouth sat on his white horse and watched him go.

Wade said that they did not attempt to pursue them 'for they had no manner of confidence in their horse.' This was Monmouth's worry all through the campaign. The cavalry were raw recruits for the most part riding untrained horses unused to the noise of battle. About eighty Royalist and eighteen rebel troops were killed. One of the rebels, a young Captain Holmes, was wounded in the arm, and, so the story goes, he cut off the damaged limb himself.

Wade continued: 'We stayed in the field until about eleven o'clock, and then leaving great fires we marched (I suppose on the advice of Colonel Venner) to Frome in a miserable rainy night up to the knees in dirt, almost to the destruction of our foot.'

Feversham wrote an apologetic letter to the King.

Sunday, 28th June.

The rebel army reached **Frome** at about 8 am. The men were put into quarters, and stayed there all that day, to refresh both them and the horses.

Monday, 29th June.

Monmouth expected to receive new recruits and stores at **Frome**, but he found neither. The Earl of Pembroke's Militia had already taken the stores, and a number of prisoners as well. Whilst the Duke was here, news arrived that the rising in Scotland had failed, and Argyll had been defeated.

Having tramped all those miles of countryside over the Mendips and down through the valleys, the army as well as its Commanders became more and more dispirited, so much so that at Frome many deserted. The leaders even discussed the possibility of fleeing to Holland, but this was opposed 'as a thing so base that it could never be forgiven by the people to be so deserted, and the Duke must never expect more to be trusted.' So – no Henrietta for the Duke!

They decided to return to Bridgwater, where they hoped ten thousand Clubmen waited to support them. The Duke gave orders for a march on Tuesday morning, which was to have been to **Warminster**, but Feversham's cavalry had reported the Duke's intention, and Feversham went south to meet them. Learning of this, Monmouth changed his plan.

Tuesday, 30th June.

The Duke avoided confrontation with the Royalist troops on the open plains of Wiltshire by going back to **Shepton Mallet**, and here his men were quartered in houses, Wade commenting, 'Here I suppose we were at free quarters, money being short.' How different were the circumstances now from their last visit. A vast number of men had deserted, their money was nearly all gone, Argyll had been executed, and still they struggled against the pitiless weather. It had never stopped raining. Colonel Venner and Major Parsons had left for the Continent, ostensibly to buy arms, and it was later reported that Colonel John Speke had gone also.

The King had published a proclamation promising pardon to all those rebels who deserted the Duke and allied themselves with the King. They were required to obtain a certificate from a local magistrate to confirm their change of heart. In the Museum at Wells is a copy of this Proclamation of the 'King's Majesties most Gracious and General pardon Given at Court at Whitehall 10th March 1685' [As the Calendar year did not coincide with today's Calendar, the Proclamation was, in today's terms issued in 1686].

Those not included in the pardon were described as follows:

> Except also all and every Person and Persons who in Traitorous and hostile manner invaded this our Realm with James Scott late Duke of Monmouth, and all and every person or persons who in the time of the late Rebellion under the said late Duke of Monmouth were officers or had the Name or Repute of being officers in his Army. Among those also 'excepted out of this our pardon' were Richard Goodenough, Nathaniel Wade, John Trenchard, Mrs. Musgrave and Robert Ferguson-Clerk.

John Coad, one of the men very badly wounded at **Norton St. Philip**, where the surgeon had refused to dress his wounds, 'being judged mortal,' was finally treated by an apothecary named Mr. Hardy who cut off his 'bloody clothes' which had stuck to his body, and took a bullet out of his back. Eventually he was re-united with his wife at **Long Sutton**, near **Langport**.

By now the Royalists were well cared for under tents, which also housed their horses. John Churchill had written to his wife telling her that they had had 'an abundance of rain,' which had tired their soldiers and prevented them from harassing the Duke of Monmouth as much as they ought to have done.

Wednesday, 1st July.

Monmouth moved on to **Wells** 'on information that there were some carriages there of the King's guarded by a small party of dragoons, which we took, and quartered there all night.' These were Kirke's waggons, which contained ammunition, arms and money – a timely boost for Monmouth's coffers.

The rebels behaved very badly in Wells. According to some reports they vandalised the Cathedral furnishings and stripped lead from the roof for bullets. The canons of Wells had already raised a hundred pounds for the King's troops, and they fled from Monmouth, leaving 'their wives to guard their homes and the Vergers to worship God.' The rebel Officer Commissionary, General Storey, took twenty pounds from the wife of a residentiary canon, threatening the Cathedral and their houses with devastation if she did not pay.

A formerly well-disciplined army was now, in the face of hunger and desperation, deteriorating. They sheltered their horses in the Cathedral, which they may have felt necessary to keep them dry, but then, it is said, 'they destroyed the furniture and organ and held a beastly orgy in the sacred place, hoisting a beer barrel on to the Holy Table, which Lord Grey defended from further insult by standing in front of it with a drawn sword..' Some later historians thought that their actions were exaggerated, but there was some substance in the complaints of the church people. The only man left in charge of the Cathedral was the Sacristan, James Williams, who very ably took the place of the Dean and Chapter by preserving the ornaments and plate inherited from the time of Queen Elizabeth I. The Dean's silver verge was the only piece lost. James Holt, Chancellor of the Cathedral, had remained, and he held a Chapter Meeting by himself on 29th July, and adjourned it for four weeks. On their return the Dean and Chapter rewarded James Williams, 'for his very honest services,' with ten pounds out of the ecclesiastical funds.

In Feversham's camp, Kirke's laxity in leaving the waggons at Wells was criticised, but he defended himself by maintaining that he had had to lend the horses to the artillery.

Thursday, 2nd July.

Having rested at Wells, the Duke led his rain-sodden forces over the wet moors towards **Bridgwater**, where he expected to meet men of the great Club Army in their thousands. Instead, he found only a gathering of about one hundred and sixty Clubmen from the marshes armed with pitchforks, flails and bludgeons. That night camp was set up on **Pedwell Plain**, a part of **Sedgemoor**.

Friday, 3rd July.

Only ten days ago the new 'King' had entered **Bridgwater** amid cheers and rejoicing, and he had received men, money and munitions.

Now he returned to be greeted by a less than enthusiastic crowd, with Earl Grey leading about five thousand men, and the Duke at the head of the Clubmen, with green boughs in their hats and a white apron for a banner. Here the rebel army refreshed themselves and 'fixed their arms which were very much out of order.'

Monmouth had to make a firm decision at this stage in his campaign. He sent Major Manley and his son to London in a forlorn hope of attracting Whig supporters, whilst his main plan was to try again to take Bristol. As a subterfuge he sent out warrants 'to summon in the country people with spades and pickaxes to work, as if we intended to fortify. Something of that nature was done, but only to secure our quarters and amuse the world, intending nothing less than to stay there.' A warrant was sent to the High Constable of Whitleigh demanding labourers, carpenters and provisions. But the town of Bridgwater was in no mood for another lengthy rebel occupation, and they gave the minimum of help.

Monmouth hoped to cross **Keynsham** bridge again with a better trained, better equipped army. He sent for new saddles and horses, and needing extra cannon, he sent to **Minehead** for six which were at the quay there. He hoped also to obtain horses and more weapons from that friendly town. He received a deputation from **Taunton** requesting him not to go back to there again in case of reprisals from the Royalists. A request of this nature was highly offensive to the Duke, who had received such acclaim there before.

Saturday, 4th July.

Monmouth spent the day exercising the troops and checking their arms, and Wade reported, 'great numbers from us went to Taunton to see their friends.' Many returned to the camp on Sunday, which showed how loyal these brave men were to the Cause.

Meanwhile Feversham's troops had arrived at **Somerton**, the ancient capital of Somerset, from **Glastonbury**, and whilst they rested there, spies were sent to see what was going on in **Bridgwater**. They reported that the rebels were indeed in the town, and 'had a barricade on the bridge, and had planted two pieces of cannon at the Cross and two in the Castle and one at the South Gate.' Feversham sent warrants to the Constables of the villages around forbidding them to supply provisions for the rebels, and then he rode through the village and over the moor to choose a site for his camp.

Sunday, 5th July.

Feversham moved his troops from **Somerton** on to the moor. Five regiments were encamped at **Pitzoy Pound** in **Zog**, in the parish of

Western Zoyland. Five hundred cavalry were stationed at the Headquarters in Weston Zoyland on slightly higher ground which was reasonably drained. They were behind the **Bussex Rhine**, a ditch which often flooded when the **River Parrett** was in flood. The Wiltshire Militia, about fifteen hundred strong, were stationed at **Middlezoy** and **Othery**, and a company of dragoons was despatched southwards to guard the crossing over the Parrett at **Burrow Bridge**. The artillery was positioned to control the road to **Bridgwater**.

The Duke heard that Feversham had reached Somerton. It was now his intention to march from Bridgwater on the following evening to **Axbridge**, cross **Keynsham** bridge and proceed not to Bristol, but north to **Gloucester** and on into Shropshire and Cheshire to join his friends there – possibly hoping to be able to escape if he failed to take his army all the way with him. His orders to his army in **Castle Field** that morning were that Taunton was to be their objective. However, the waggons and guns had been moved to the Keynsham road, giving Churchill's spies an insight into Monmouth's intentions. Churchill, knowing Monmouth well, warned that the Duke might take this course of action.

In Monmouth's camp rebel soldiers were returning from their visit to their families, many bringing their wives with them, and the town was thronged with women and children saying their last farewells. Despite the melancholy of these partings, there was a new sense of purpose, even of exhilaration in the air.

Among a number of interesting relics in the Somerset County Museum in Taunton Castle is the spy-glass through which a William Sparke observed, from Chedzoy Church tower, the approach of the King's troops. He is said to have reported to Monmouth at Bridgwater that they were carelessly encamped around Weston Zoyland. Another story states that at about 3 p.m., as Monmouth was crossing the town

Spy glass allegedly used by William Sparke on Chedzoy Church tower to observe the movements of the King's troops. *Photograph by courtesy of the Somerset County Museum.*

St. Mary's Church, Bridgwater. From the tower Monmouth and Lord Grey are said to have watched the King's troops on Sedgemoor, and recognised Lord Dumbarton's Regiment.

bridge towards the camp in Castle Field, he encountered a young cow-herd, Richard Godfrey, whose father lived at Sutton Mallet near Weston Zoyland, close to where Feversham had pitched his camp. He told the Duke exactly where Feversham's emplacements were. Monmouth sent Godfrey to find out more about the camp, and, together with Lord Grey and other officers, climbed the tower of **Bridgwater Church** to survey the Royalist camp with a spy-glass. He recognised Lord Dumbarton's Regiment, of which he himself had once been Colonel, which was now stationed on the side of the camp where he might attack. He was concerned at this, and said: "I know these men

41

will fight, and if I had them I would not doubt of success."

Godfrey returned and told Monmouth that there were no entrenchments, but he failed to mention the state of the Bussex Rhine, which was very wet and miry. There were two simple bridges or 'Plungeons' over this watercourse. The King's men were 'enjoying their rest and fuddling themselves with Zoyland cider.' Richard Godfrey was quite confident that he could lead Monmouth and his forces over the moor. The Duke gave him 'a guinea for his pains.'

Monmouth conferred with his officers on the possibility of attacking Feversham's troops, and they decided on a surprise attack at night. They planned to move round **Chedzoy** village, make a wide sweep to the north-east, and attack the rear of the enemy's right flank. Grey and the cavalry were detailed to set fire to Weston Zoyland village in the rear where the Royalist cavalry were billeted, and during the confusion the foot would attack the main army in the front of the village. Monmouth would lead a second body of foot up from the moor, and three guns would follow the cavalry. With great optimism the Duke said, 'we shall have no more to do than to lock up the troopers in their beds.' He had been urged by Colonel Mathews to divide Lord Grey's cavalry into two parts, so that if one group ran away the army would still have cavalry support, but lacking the hardness in his nature to do this, he refused, saying that he did not wish to 'affront my Lord.'

In the evening the rattling drums summoned the troops to Castle Field, where Ferguson preached to them, taking his text from Joshua 22: 'The Lord God of Hosts knoweth and Israel he shall know if it be in rebellion or in transgression against the Lord, save us not this day.' A young Bridgwater girl, having heard of Monmouth's plan of attack, walked to the Royalist camp to warn Feversham: 'Lord Feversham,' it was said, 'instead of listening to what she had to say, offered her violence, and in her rage she concealed what she had come to divulge.'

She might well have put a curse on Feversham, for those were days of great superstition. The rector of Chedzoy, Reverend Andrew Paschall, had warned London of troubles to come, for he had observed strange happenings which had augured ill for the people. In 1680 siamese twins were born; the following year there came an earthquake – 'This motion was observed in Bridgwater, Taunton, Wells and other places near some caverns in the Mendip Hill.' Monmouth should have taken heed of a gypsy who had warned him, 'Beware of the Rhine,' but at that time he had probably never heard of the Bussex Rhine on **Sedgemoor**.

At the news of the impending attack the rebels rejoiced that there would at last be some action to support the Protestant Cause.

A Sedgemoor rhine.

Nevertheless, the lack of support from the gentry still rankled. As some had said when they were last in Bridgwater, 'We wonder the gentlemen come not in. Well, we will do the work without them, and then we will have their estates too.'

At about 11 p.m. Feversham made his last tour of inspection of the Royalist Camp and went to bed. At about the same time Monmouth prepared to leave Bridgwater to mount the attack. The password, 'So-ho', the traditional hunting call, had a double meaning – Monmouth's house was in London's Soho Square. It was demolished in 1773.

Night March on Sedgemoor

Sunday 5th July

As the bright full moon rose it was gradually covered by a curtain of thick mist drifting from the moor, and Monmouth, an observer noted, 'had an alteration in his look which I did not like.' The Duke was taking a great risk in involving his rustic rebels in a night attack, which would have been difficult even for seasoned forces. By now, however, he had become adept at night excursions, so on foot, and carrying an officer's half-pike, he led his men, under pain of death to break the muffled silence, down the **Eastern Causeway,** from Bridgwater and then along a narrow lane which ran towards **The Polden Hills**, this being the road to Bristol in 1685.

Map of Sedgemoor. From George Roberts, 'Life of Monmouth'.

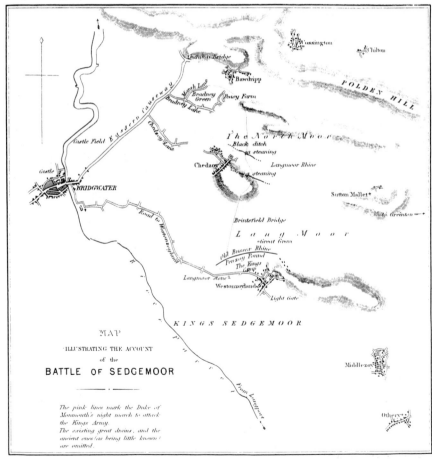

Peazey Farm near Bawdrip, Sedgemoor.

Entering **Bradney Lane**, also known as **War Lane**, they quietly avoided the house of a known Royalist supporter and then turned into **Marsh Lane**, moving in a north-easterly direction. A Royalist guard was stationed in **Chedzoy** village, which the Duke again avoided, and then they were struggling along the tracks and paths and lanes of the marsh with their horses and weapons. Keeping silent under these conditions, especially as they had bolstered their courage with cider from the town, was a feat of endurance; normally the sentries would have been alerted throughout the area at the passage of a mile-long column of some five thousand men with their accoutrements and weapons, and horses by the hundred. Only the soft going underfoot on the spongy damp peat marsh made possible this march which, astonishingly enough, was not detected by the enemy.

They continued in this manner towards **Weston Zoyland** until a little before **Peazey Farm**, which was on higher ground near **Bawdrip**. Here they halted to allow Lord Grey and his five hundred cavalry to get ahead of the main force and be in position to attack the Royalist cavalry to the rear of the village, as they had planned, and 'that the Canon should follow the horse, and the foot the Canon, and draw all up in one line and so finish what the horse had begun before the King's horse or canon could get in order.' Reaching Peazey Farm was of great importance to their guide, Godfrey, for from here he could get his bearings. Here the Duke ordered the forty-two baggage waggons to remain until they heard the guns, and then drive on to **Axbridge**.

King's Sedgemoor Drain, partly on the line of the old Black Ditch.

Colonel Oglethorpe was out with a Royalist patrol on reconnaissance along the roads north of Bridgwater at this time, but he saw nothing of their movements, although the King's men did discover later that Bridgwater had been evacuated.

The rebel forces steathily followed their guide on to the open moor. He confidently found the ford over the **Black Ditch** near **Parchey** which the army crossed successfully. Suddenly, at the sound of cavalry, they stood stock still in the mist, and an enemy troop passed on the further side of what is now **King's Sedgemoor Drain** without seeing them. A party of Royalist cavalry had been in the area 'by Langmoor Stone and step stones to Parchey Gate,' and guards and sentries had been placed in all the avenues, including the Langmoor Stone, 'but all were gone at bedtime.'

By this time the Royalist forces had settled down for the night: 'Their camp in Zog consisting of five regiments was at rest in the tents, the muskets and pikes standing up against them. The Lord General was on his campaign bed set up in the parlour at Weston Court.'

Colonel Kirke's lodgings were at **Weston Zoyland Vicarage** – unusual surroundings considering his views on religion. Although he was a corrupt and brutal man, he had an engaging manner and a dry sense of humour. He was popular with the King. Trying to convert him to the Roman Catholic faith, King James once said, "Kirke, you do not mind religion. Why cannot you be of mine as well as another?."

"Sir, I am very sorry for to be pre-engaged."

"To whom?"

Copy of an illustration of the Battle of Sedgemoor now in Weston Zoyland Church.

"When I had the honour to command at Tangiers, I promised the King of Morocco that if I ever I changed my religion, I would become a Mohammedan."

The Bishop of Winchester, Peter Mews, known as 'Old Patch', or the 'Bombardier Bishop', was with the King's men, and stayed at the house of a man called Baker.

Monmouth's army having crossed the first ditch at Parchey, his plans seemed to be going well. There were those who knew what was afoot.

'Countrymen, hearing that the Duke was moving, informed divers of the officers of the King's soldiers of it,' but apparently little notice was taken of them. Then the thick, drenching mist closed over the moor and the rebel force groping their way over the sticky peat marshes.

The Sedgemoor Battlefield today.

In trying to keep well to the east of Chedzoy, where some of the Royalist cavalry were stationed, Godfrey missed the waterway crossing at **Langmoor Stone** [also known as the Devil's Upping Stone: since destroyed], and in his effort to find the stepping stones he caused confusion among the weary, stumbling men who were dragging their horses over the bog, and then found themselves struggling through deep water and the muddy bottom of the **Langmoor Rhine**. Amid the confusion and delay Godfrey finally found the ford, but the men were now hampered by the lack of communication imposed by the restrictions of their enforced silence, and there was a halt whilst the army regrouped and the cavalry scrambled out of the muddy swamp of the Rhine. Well indeed had Monmouth been warned, 'Beware of the Rhine.' Suddenly a pistol shot pierced the mist-shrouded moor, and with more than a mile yet to go, all surprise was lost.

The trooper of the Royal Blues who fired the shot – although Daniel Defoe, who was with Monmouth's army, states that it was a rebel who did so – sped off to **Chedzoy** to warn his troop Commander, Sir Francis Compton, and called at least twenty times to Dumbarton's Royal Scots by the Bussex Rhine: "Beat your drums, the enemy is come. For Lord's sake, beat your drums!" Dumbarton, who had anticipated that Monmouth would attack in this way, was ready for him: 'Now the drums beat, the drummers running to it, even bare foot for haste. All fly for arms. All are drawn out of their tents and in five battalions stand in the space between the tents and the ditch.'

The battle began between 1 and 2 a.m. on 6th July. Monmouth had a superiority in numbers, but they were raw and untrained. Some of his cavalry under Captain Jones, formerly a cabinet maker, had a sharp encounter by the upper plungeon, or rough bridge, over the Bussex Rhine, which was guarded by Compton's detachment, and during the exchange of pistol and carbine shots Jones was wounded, but gallantly fought on. His troop fought well, but could not overcome the three troops of seasoned men of the Royal army, and these rebels retreated to Sutton Mallet.

Monmouth, realising that the whole camp had been aroused, ordered Lord Grey to press on with all haste and 'fall in among the tents and take them in the flank.' With his five hundred horsemen Grey did press on, but instead of riding further eastward to cross the Rhine at the upper plungeon, he missed this bridge, and led his men along the bank of the ditch until he was opposite Dumbarton's force. From the misty darkness they were challenged, and said they were from Albemarle, and they came across in front of the Royalists. Another challenge came:

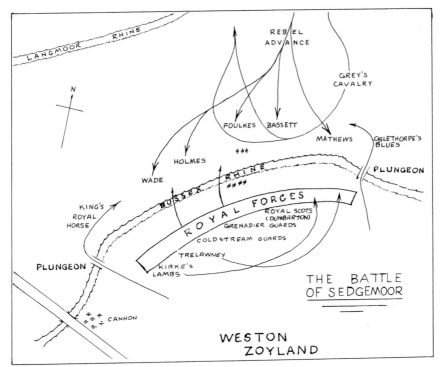

Sketch of the Battle positions.

"Who are you for?" shouted the Royalists.

"Monmouth, and God be with us!" they answered.

"Take this with you then," was the reply, and a volley was fired into their ranks.

More volleys followed whilst Grey and his men struggled to control their horses, terrified by the din. Many of the riders were wounded or thrown from their mounts, confusion arose among them, and the raw horses stampeded under the hail of fire from the enemy. Grey's men wheeled and galloped back across the front of the rebel foot, skirmishing in the confusion with their own troops who were advancing at speed with Monmouth at their head: 'Thus a consternation went into the hinder part of the Duke's army which, by the narrowness of the lanes retarding them, were not come up.'

The night battle, with the crashing fire of the cannon and the flashes from the musketry, was altogether too much for the 'ragged horse,' and finally they all vanished into the mist and the darkness in headlong retreat.

49

Seeing his cavalry retreating in such disarray, the Duke speedily brought up towards the 'King's Camp' his infantry regiments, together with the 'three little cannon.' Colonel Wade, with great aplomb, led the Red Regiment across the moor, and battalion after battalion were, in the darkness, guided into position opposite Dumbarton's regiment by the glow of the enemy's matches. He calmly ordered his battle lines, ordering his troops to hold their fire until all was ready. Before the first three battalions were properly in line, Mathews with the Yellow Regiment next on his flank, without orders from his Colonel, began firing, and then Wade's and Holmes' regiment did likewise.

But the rebel soldiers would not advance across the Rhine to engage the enemy at close quarters, nor even approach more than thirty or forty paces from their bank of the waterway. Blazing away with their muskets, they shot too high, and fired over the heads of the kneeling troops opposite. They did some damage to the rear ranks of Dumbarton's Scots, but his front ranks held their position 'with great order and steadiness'. The firing went on for some thirty minutes, using ammunition at such a rate that they were demanding more – "Ammunition, ammunition! For the Lord's sake, ammunition!"

The splendid Dutch Master Gunner directed his cannon accurately, and, as King James later observed, his fire was 'very well plied, and did great execution on Douglas and the first battalion of the Guards...which lost many officers and soldiers, and most of them by cannon.' The rebel forces held their ground, but would advance no further. All but four of Lieutenant Colonel Douglas's Royalist force were injured or killed. Churchill, without waiting for orders, bolstered up the Royalist's right flank and brought Kirke's and Trelawney's Tangier Regiment to the right of the Scots Regiment.

The cannon were firing with devastating accuracy, but Wade now urgently needed ammunition, and was agonisingly calling for more. The baggage men and their ammunition waggons, slowly following from **Peazey Farm**, were mixed up with the frantic mass of riderless horses and fugitives that had been Grey's cavalry, fleeing as fast as they could, and the drivers, alarmed by the arrival of the panic-stricken horsemen, believed that the army had been routed, and turned away and followed the fleeing mob towards **Ware** and **Axbridge**. The next day, all the waggons were captured by the King's men.

By now, the mist was beginning to clear over the battlefield as Dumbarton's men fell back, their guns out of action from the formidable fire of the Dutchman's three little cannon. At this point, timely reinforcements in the shape of troops led by 'Old Patch,' the Bombardier Bishop, arrived. In the absence of ready artillery horses he

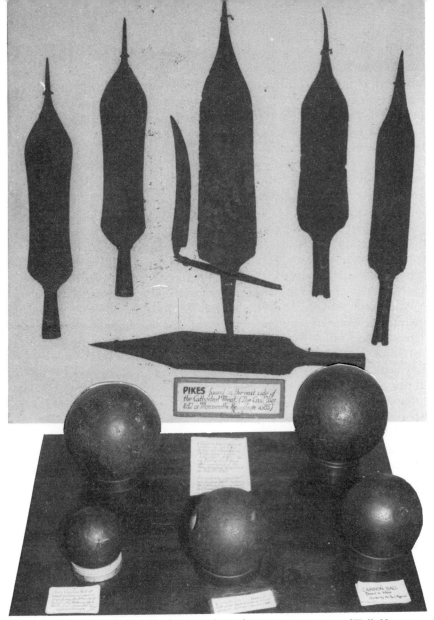

Weapons and cannon-balls of the kind used at Sedgemoor. *By courtesy of Wells Museum.*

brought his coach horses, which sturdily dragged six guns over the boggy ground to the support of the Scots on the Bussex Rhine.

Monmouth, in support of Wade still gallantly fighting on the bank of the Bussex Rhine, brought up more infantry, including the scythmen, who had been held in reserve. These men with their sharpened scythes

51

— 'murderous weapons,' said the Royalists — fearlessly followed the Duke, who was armed with a pike. The Royalist soldiers had now swarmed over the water and the mud to attack them, and the Duke led his men in a last forlorn hope into the field of writhing bodies locked in hand-to-hand fighting. Devastated by the artillery fire, the scythe and pitchfork rebels fought fanatically, but the three little cannon were finally silenced and captured.

Lord Feversham had by now arisen from his bed, found his wig, adjusted his cravat at a 'paltry mirror' and emerged to order his forces and move in to crush the rebels. The pale light of dawn had begun to filter over the battlefield.

Feversham sent Oglethorpe's cavalry across the upper Rhine to reconnoitre the ground in front of his right flank, and here he met a small remnant of Monmouth's cavalry. After a brief encounter the rebels retreated, but the King's men were halted. Feversham, not knowing what had happened to Monmouth's forces, ordered his troops to wheel to the left and to keep their ground, unwilling to attack the infantry whilst there might be the chance of a cavalry counter-attack. This was too much for Oglethorpe, and he attacked the nearest rebel battalion. Colonel Holmes fought back strongly and beat back the Royalists, who had several men wounded and knocked off their horses in the desperate hand-to-hand fighting.

Against the increasing Royalist pressure the rebel flanks were breaking, but Monmouth pressed on into the fight, where he was shortly joined by Earl Grey, who had returned to the battle and fought his way to the Duke's side. The peasants thrust forward their scythes and pitchforks and swung their bludgeons against the hard steel of their enemies' weapons, fighting sturdily against heavy odds. 'Even in the extremity,' wrote Macauley, 'the Mendip miners stood bravely to their arms, and sold their lives dearly.'

Feversham ordered his infantry across the Rhine, and the rebel battalion broke and fled. Wade had held his position up to that point. He recorded: 'We continued in that station, firing for about an hour and a half, when, it being pretty light, I perceived all the Battalions on the left running (who I since understood were broken by the King's horse of the left wing), and finding my own men not inclined to stand, I caused them to face about and make a kind of disorderly retreat to a ditch a great way behind us, where we were charged by a party of horse and dragoons and routed: about one hundred and fifty getting over the ditch, I marched with them to Bridgwater.'

There he found the fugitive cavalry, amongst whom was Ferguson. He went on northwards, and met the troops who had been sent to

Late 17th century playing card, showing the cannon taken and Monmouth's men in flight.

Minehead for cannon. With about fifty of these he proceeded to **Ilfracombe**, where they seized a ship and put to sea, but they were forced ashore by two frigates which were cruising the coast, and they dispersed into the woods.

On the battlefield in the midst of the rout, Williams, Monmouth's steward, pointed out that the King's cavalry were about to surround them. The Duke stripped off his armour, took a hundred guineas from his steward and, together with Lord Grey, Buyse, 'the Brandenburger' and Dr Oliver, turned to leave the battlefield. Asked to stay and encourage the men in the field against the King's troops he replied: "All the world cannot stop those fellows; they will run presently."

He then ran himself. He reached **Brinsfield Bridge**, and stopped at **Chedzoy**, where he was supplied with another horse.

William Stradling, writing in 1839, related: 'The horse was the property of an ancestor of mine, and tradition says that whilst the servant was putting on the saddle and bridle, the Duke stepped into the house and took off his collar and George. He had round his neck what appeared to be a lady's girdle, of blue ribbon richly embroidered, and fastened with a silver buckle. This he threw over the neck of a little boy two years old, whom he took in his arms and kissed, saying, "This may be of use to you some day, and I can have it again." For many years afterwards this curious relic was touched by the superstitious for the King's Evil. When the proprietor was married he settled in Barnstaple, where he died. The ribbon was lost, but I still have the buckle.' A buckle is now in the Taunton Museum.

The Duke went on over **Crandon Bridge** and the **Polden Hills**, and across the **Mendip Hills** to **Downside** near Shepton Mallet, where he sheltered for the night with Edward Strode.

On the battlefield – leaderless, mown down by the Royalist artillery

Memorial on burial ground to those slain at Sedgemoor, 6th July, 1685.

Inscription on Memorial stone at Sedgemoor.

TO THE GLORY OF GOD
AND IN MEMORY OF ALL THOSE WHO
DOING THE RIGHT AS THEY GAVE IT
FELL IN THE BATTLE OF SEDGEMOOR
6th JVLY 1685
AND LIE BVRIED IN THIS FIELD
OR WHO FOR THEIR SHARE IN THE FIGHT
SVFFERED DEATH
PVNISHMENT OR TRANSPORTATION
PRO PATRIA

and attacked from all sides by Churchill's forces – the rebels were pursued by Kirke's infantry and dragoons, who slaughtered them without mercy by bullet and sword. The greatest killing took place along the deep and boggy ditch of **Langmoor Rhine** and in the fields of ripening corn beside the battlefield. Weary fugitives fleeing from the strife and bloodshed staggered, wounded and terror-stricken, towards a hope of shelter in the town of Bridgwater. They were mercilessly pursued.

So ended the last battle on English soil.

Signboard of the Sedgemoor Inn, Weston Zoyland.

Monday, 6th July.

More than a thousand rebels were killed in the action. The heavy Royalist losses, some four hundred, enraged their leaders, 'for Kirke and others slew the fugitives and prisoners with great cruelty, and are said to have buried the wounded with the dead in clearing up the battlefield.'

The parish register of **Weston Zoyland** contained the following entry, which appeared in a work entitled 'Chilton Priory' published at Bridgwater in 1839, 'being the account of the fight in Langmoor, 6th of July 1685.':

'There was killed on the spot of the King's soldiers sixteen, and five of them buried in the Church, the rest in the Churchyard; and they all had a Christian burial. One hundred or more of the King's soldiers wounded, of which wounds many died; of which we have no certain account. There was killed of the rebels upon the spot about 300; hanged with us 22, or which 4 were hanged in gemmaces [*chains*]. About 500 prisoners brought into our church; of which there was 79 wounded, and 5 of them died of wounds in our church.'

How long the prisoners remained in the Church is not known, but it ultimately had to be disinfected with frankincense, resin and saltpetre.

The drummer who beat the alarm when the rebels came to battle, Adam Wheeler of the Wiltshire Militia, wrote an account of the way in which the prisoners were brutally brought in from the battlefield. He had seen one hundred and seventy four dead buried in a mass grave. He sat writing the numbers on his drumhead as the prisoners, mostly tied together, came into Weston Zoyland church. Eyes glazed with fear looked out piteously from drawn faces as they entered. The first group numbered fifty-five and the second thirty-two, and they were followed by two crawling on hands and knees, one stripped to his drawers and another forced to run by two horsemen who were beating him. The total on Wheeler's drumhead finally was two hundred and thirty-eight.

'Such of them as had a good coat or anything worth the Pilling were fairly stripped of it,' he wrote.

The last prisoner, wounded and alone, whose 'pathos' may be remembered for all time, was, Wheeler said, 'very remarkable and to be admired, for being shot through the Shoulder and wounded in the Belly, he lay on his Back in the sun stript naked, for the space of ten or eleven hours in that scorching hot day, to the Admiration of all the Spectators; and as he lay, a great Crowd of Soldiers came about him and reproached him, calling him "Thou Monmouth Dog. How long have you been with your King Monmouth?" His answer was that if he had Breath he would tell them. Afterwards he was pitied, and they opened

Weston Zoyland Church.

Interior of Westonzoyland Church.

round about him and gave him more libery of the Aire, and there was one Soldier that gave him a pair of drawers to cover his nakedness: Afterwards, having a long stick in his hand, he walked feebly to Weston Church where he died that night, and two wounded men more.'

One of those hanged was a valiant Dutch gunner, and another was 'Captain Adlam, who was so severely wounded that he was in a dying state when taken to the gallows the next day, and the first who was hung in chains on the moor. He had a hundred broad pieces quilted in his buff coat. The other eighteen who were hung, in the absence of gallows, were suspended on the branches of a large tree at Bussex, adjoining the moor, and their bodies were buried near it by some of the cottagers.'

Some prisoners escaped through the cornfield, and the corpses of other rebels who had died of wounds lay in the corn until it was reaped in the autumn.

The bells in every village around were rung in celebration, but there was hardly a home in that part of the West Country that did not mourn the dead, or fear for what lay ahead. The farmers in the neighbouring villages sent hogsheads of cider to the victors, having inscribed on them their names, and those of their farms.

Thomas Dare, the Mayor of Lymington, fled for his life. Lymington Town Records show in 1686: 'Beer to the Ringers, Thanksgiving Day [*for the battle of Sedgemoor*] ...0. 5s 6d.' but no signature was appended – as was usual – by the Mayor. Since the Bloody Assize was then sitting, perhaps the local people, many of whom were of the Whig complexion, were reluctant to attend the parish meeting.

Many legends were associated with the activities of the soldiers and the people after the battle. Whilst Feversham was 'entertaining himself with the execution of the prisoners,' many of his officers returned to Weston Zoyland and pushed their way into different houses in the village and ordered refreshment. One ill-bred ruffian entered the home of the Bridge family, which had recently been the Headquarters of his General. He swaggered through the great hall to the parlour where the ladies were, and using foul language, he finally offered 'a gross insult' to the lady of the mansion, whereupon her eleven-year-old daughter Mary drew his sword and 'stabbed him to the heart.'

She was brought before Colonel Kirke to be tried by court martial, where the fair young heroine was not only honourably acquitted, but it was ordered that the sword should be given to her, and that it should descend to the future Mary Bridges of the family.

It was told of Kirke that 'he promised to save the lover of a beautiful woman if she would spend the night with him, and in that morning he

Mary Bridge's sword, and Captain Durston's pistol used at Sedgemoor.
Photograph by courtesy of the Somerset County Museum.

drew the curtain of the window and showed his companion her lover hanging in the courtyard of the inn.' Although this was 'not proven' against Kirke, it is not uncharacteristic of the man.

Another episode shows the manner in which a young ensign was treated. He was offered his life if he would race a wild colt from the marsh. The youth allowed himself to be stripped, and he was then attached by a halter round the neck to a young colt. They started off at speed from **Bussex Rhine** and ran until the colt fell exhausted by the side of the young ensign by **Brinsfield Bridge** in **Chedzoy** parish, a distance of three quarters of a mile. The ensign claimed his life, but the Royalist officer ordered him to be hanged with the rest, and his body was flung into the common grave.

The villagers told afterwards of the 'White Lady of Zoyland,' his sweetheart, who died of grief and was said to haunt the great grave, mourning her lover.

A story with a happier ending concerns John Swain, an athletic young man from **Shapwick**, near Glastonbury, who was arrested in his bed a few nights after the battle by two of Kirke's dragoons. As they were marching him off to Bridgwater they were followed by his wife and young children. At **Loxley Wood** he begged to be allowed to show his children his prowess as a jumper so that they could have something by which to remember him, and his request was granted. To the astonishment of the soldiers he ran, took three enormous leaps, and disappeared into the thickly wooded coppice and swamps where it was impossible for the horsemen to follow. When it was safe for him to do so, he returned to his wife and family, and 'Swain's Leap' was marked by stones.

Another escape occurred when Richard Cogan, of **Coaxdon Hall** near Axminster, fled for shelter at the **Green Dragon** in Axminster. The innkeeper's daughter, Elizabeth Gray, rushed him upstairs and pushed him face-downwards on a bed, covering him with a feather mattress. Then re-arranging the bedclothes 'so deftly,' she continued with her chores. Although the pursuing soldiers twice searched the room, even under the bed, they failed to find him. After the General Pardon was declared in the early part of 1686 he returned to marry his Elizabeth.

They were cruel times, and the hangings continued. Many spectators attended the executions voluntarily, but others were ordered by Kirke to be present, and to drink to the health of King James as the drums rolled for the execution.

Swain's Leap, an engraving from the 'Life of Monmouth'.

Tuesday, 7th July.

The Wiltshire Militia, leaving **Sedgemoor** for home, marched to **Glastonbury**, where six rebels were hanged from the sign of the **White Hart Inn**. Adam Wheeler wrote that they were stripped naked and left hanging by the Militia when they left for Wells.

Meanwhile, the Duke of Monmouth was entertained at **Downside** by Edward Strode, who had previously supplied money for his campaign. [Strode would not suffer for his part in the rebellion, but received a King's Pardon, for which, no doubt, he paid heavily.] Dr Oliver, Monmouth's physician, left the party here. He parted from the Duke with tears in his eyes, for he felt that they would never meet again. He made his way to **Bristol**, where he was received by friends, one of whom, a good Tory, introduced him to, of all people, Judge Jeffreys' clerk, with whom he travelled to London and then made his way to Holland. He ended a noted medical career as physician to the Royal Hospital at Bath, and is buried in the Abbey Church there.

The Duke and his friends Lord Grey and Buyse 'the Brandenburger' left in the early morning, leaving behind them two horse pistols in their hurry. They went through **Selwood Forest** and on across the quiet countryside on the borders of Somerset and Wiltshire, keeping away from the towns and villages and following the lonely forest tracks to enter Dorset near to **Gillingham**. They intended to try to make contact with Colonel Dare, the Mayor of **Lymington** on the Solent side of the New Forest, who might perhaps provide a ship for the continent, or to turn towards the Puritan town of **Poole**, and sail from there for Holland.

In **Bridgwater**, Churchill had patrolled the area with five hundred cavalry and an equal number of foot to quell any further opposition, but there appear to have been no atrocities under his command. The town was empty of rebels, and Oglethorpe was ordered to London with news of the victory. Churchill brought many more wounded rebels in carts to **Weston Zoyland**, and the next day on Feversham's orders men were strung from a long line of gibbets from Bridgwater to Weston Zoyland.

The Wiltshire Militia, under Colonel Wyndham, rested at **Wells**, where they were received by the jubilant clergy. At a church parade 'Old Patch' preached to both the soldiers and their prisoners – the last taste of the blessings of religion for five unfortunate rebels who were hanged before the Cathedral which had been the scene of desecration barely a week before. The Militia then continued on their way to **Norton St. Philip**. Meanwhile Kirke zealously and efficiently combed the towns, the villages and the surrounding countryside for remaining rebels, who were herded into Bridgwater. His 'Lambs' scoured the West Country for rebels hiding in cornfields and copses, or cowering in hidden rooms in houses and in barns and stables. Many were betrayed by their friends.

Some were lucky, like John Clapp, a mercer of **Colyton** in Devon, who had reached home after the battle and fallen into bed. He heard the soldiers coming, and hastily climbed through a trap door in his ceiling. The soldiers found a warm bed, and searched for him, but 'they failed to notice the trap door, and gave up the search.'

Another Colyton man, Zachary Drower, was not so lucky. He hid under a water mill: 'The searchers, having searched the premises unsuccessfully, were moving off when one of them noticed under the wheel something white, which proved to be his sleeve, and thus led to his discovery.' However, Zachary, a joiner, was eventually pardoned and set free.

Monmouth pushed on for Hampshire, hoping for shelter in 'the cabins of the deer stealers among the oaks of the New Forest till means of conveyance to the Continent could be procured.' The three fugitives continued to ride all day through the forest byways amongst the deer in the forest which 'stretched then from the banks of the Avon in Wiltshire to the Southern Coast of Hampshire.'

In this wild, lonely country north of **Shaftesbury** they found a guide, Richard Hollyday, to lead them along a quiet route through **Cranborne Chase**. He is reported to have taken them 'through **White Sheet**, four miles east of Shaftesbury, and **Winkelbury Hill** down to **Woodyates Inn**, which is on the road between Salisbury and Blandford.'

Woodyates Inn, demolished in the 1950s, was an old posting house on the long straight road across Cranborne Chase, half a mile from the point where the counties of Dorset, Hampshire and Wiltshire meet.

It is believed to be here that Monmouth and his companions disguised themselves in rough shepherd's clothes, concealed their saddles and bridles and turned their weary horses loose. Monmouth had several days' growth of beard to help his disguise. He, with Grey and Buyse, walked furtively on through the damp undergrowth, and followed the hedges until they came to **Cranborne**. Two miles to the south lay **Wimborne St Giles**, the country seat of Lord Shaftesbury, well known to Monmouth in the past. The 'shepherds' parted here, thinking no doubt that they would have a greater chance of escape if they went separate ways. They spent the night sleeping in the rough countryside.

All the time the whole of a large area there was alive with search

Woodyates Inn: Monmouth's last stop as a free man.

parties combing the forest and the country surrounding the fugitives. Richard, Lord Lumley, based at Ringwood with the Sussex Militia, had his men thoroughly patrolling the fields and scouring the houses. Macauley said, 'William Portman, with the Sussex Militia, formed a chain of posts from the sea to the northern extremity of Dorset.'

Early in the morning of 7th July two yokels were seized at the crossroads near **Holt Lodge**, between **Wimborne** and **Ringwood**, by two of the Sussex scouts. They were Earl Grey and Hollyday, the guide. Grey submitted to his fate with calmness.

"Since we landed," he said, "I have not had one comfortable meal or one quiet night."

Lord Lumley, sensing that Monmouth could not be far from Grey, ordered an intense search of the cottages, woods and fields nearby as they redoubled their efforts to find the Duke. Monmouth and Buyse were wearily pushing their way through bracken and brambles in the thickets surrounding patches of heathland. They clambered over a hedge which bordered ragged, ill-kept plots of cultivated land, 'some overgrown by ferns and brakes and others sown with rye, peas, oats etc.'

Inexorably the militia closed in on the fugitives. Several dogs 'quick of scent' were let loose among the bushes. Each time the two men ventured to emerge from their hiding place in the bracken they were seen, and finally they were fired upon, and dared not come out into the open at all. A poor woman, Amy Farrant, who lived nearby, told the soldiers who came to her cottage that she had seen two men climb over a hedge, and that they were lurking about near there.

64

The Monmouth Ash.

The Capture of the Ragged Duke

Wednesday, 8th July.

Monmouth and Buyse had become separated in their efforts to hide in the dank, overgrown ditches. Early on the Wednesday morning Buyse was captured, and confessed that he had been with the Duke very recently, 'whereupon each individual, being encouraged thereby, and by the hopes of having a share in the five thousand pounds (as was agreed on the field), did renew the pursuit of him by the strictest search and diligence imaginable; and about seven o'clock of the same morning, one Harry Parkin happened to discover the late duke, hidden in a ditch, covered with fern and bracken; and calling two of the Sussex troopers who were by him, all three seized him together.'

The spot, since known as **Monmouth Ash**, was on the north-west edge of **Horton Heath**, at Ordnance Survey map reference SU 061 072, half a mile north of the road across the heath from **Horton** to **Three Legged Cross**. It lies 500 feet west of what is now **Monmouth Ash Farm**, midway between the farm and **Peat's Hill**.

The Duke, a haggard, hunted man, utterly exhausted, was hidden in a deep ditch under an ash tree. He was dressed in the shepherd's clothing, 'His beard, prematurely grey, was of several days' growth. He

Plaque on the Monmouth Ash.

Portrait of Monmouth wearing the George. Engraved by H. Robinson, from 'Life of Monmouth' by George Roberts.

trembled greatly, and was unable to speak. Even those who had often seen him were at first in doubt whether this were, truly, the brilliant and graceful Monmouth.'

He looked so terrible that Sir William Portman had to restrain Parkin and the other militiamen from shooting him there and then.

They searched his pockets and found 'among some raw peas gathered in a rage of hunger, a watch, a purse of gold, a small treatise on fortification, an album filled with songs, receipts, prayers and charms, and the George with which, many years ago, King Charles had

Holt Lodge, Dorset, home of Anthony Ettricke, J.P. in 1685.

decorated his favourite son.' The Duke had dropped his snuff box, full of gold pieces, in a pea field, where it was later found.

Lord Lumley was given £5000 to be shared amongst the people 'that discovered and took the late Duke of Monmouth and brought him to his said Majesty.' A further reward of £500 was shared for the capture of Lord Grey. The guide who had brought the fugitives as far as Ringwood was 'to be whipt twice, fined, and to find sureties for the good behaviour for a year.' Amy Farrant's cottage now had a curse upon it according to the superstitious locals, and they would not go near 'that place of ill omen.' Among records of the King's Secret Service was, 'To Amy Farrant, bounty of £50 for giving notice to the Lord Lumley where the Duke of Monmouth lay concealed, whereby he was apprehended.'

Ettricke's tomb in the wall of Wimborne Minster.

Following defeat at the Battle of Sedgemoor in 1685 The Duke of Monmouth was held in this house prior to his execution in the Tower of London

The 'Monmouth House', Ringwood, Dorset. Here Monmouth was held on his way to London on 8-9th July, 1685.

Once identified, the Duke was taken to **Holt Lodge** and interviewed by Anthony Ettricke, a magistrate who owned the house and who was in 1703 buried in a recess in the wall of the Holy Trinity Chapel of **Wimborne Minster**, where his tomb may still be seen. Messengers were instantly sent to Whitehall with the news, together with the George. The prisoner was taken to **Ringwood** where he stayed for two nights, the 8th and 9th of July. There is now a commemorative plaque on "Monmouth House" in Ringwood.

Monmouth employed his time in writing letters. He wrote to his uncle, King James II, repenting of what he had done and begging him for mercy:

'I hope, Sir, God Almighty will strike your heart with mercy and compassion for me, as He has done mine with the abhorrence of

69

what I have done. Wherefore, Sir, I hope I may live to show you how zealous I shall ever be for your service; and could I say but one word in this letter you would be convinced of it; but it is of that consequence that I dare not do it.'

Monmouth's signature on a letter which he wrote to the Queen Dowager from Ringwood on 9th July, 1685.

He also begged for a private audience of the King. To that same end he sent letters to the Queen Dowager and to Lord Roberts, the King's brother-in-law, imploring them to intercede for him. He did not forget friends who had helped him, and according to the **Lymington** Town Registers of 1686, wrote 'an autograph letter to some of the Knapton family – a dangerous missive which, mentioning the names of individuals, was soon destroyed.' The Knaptons lived at **Brockenhurst Manor**. A story is told of a group of Monmouth's supporters meeting at Mrs. Knapton's house who were warned of soldiers approaching. They rapidly dispersed, and all that the soldiers found was 'an old lady with her head enveloped in a flannel petticoat smoking a pipe to cure inveterate toothache.'

Thursday 9th July.

In the West Country, Kirke's Lambs continued to hunt their terrified prey, and marched a long train of manacled prisoners from **Bridgwater** to **Taunton** where, without trial, nineteen of them were hanged. The Vicar of St Mary Magdalene interred ten 'rebel soldiers,' and at the Church of St James nine more were buried. The parson there took the trouble to enter their names in the Parish Register, with the note, 'Executed for treason against His Majesty.' The Militia were re-organised to search throughout the county for rebels. Wade was captured as he came out of John Birch's house at **Brendin** in the county of Devon, and Lord Sunderland committed him to the Tower. He wrote a confession which, he was given to understand, would save his life if he would implicate plenty of people in it. He set about gaining information of men who had died at **Sedgemoor** from his friends and relations who took his washing from the Tower, and they concealed lists of names in the folds of his shirts, which names he assiduously entered in his confession. "Your friends, Mr. Wade, seem to be among the dead," said King James when interrogating the prisoner. His life was spared however.

Now that the campaign was virtually over, the army and most of the Militia were dispersed to their various bases. Feversham and his Guards and Cavalry moved to **Frome** and then to **Warminster**, and finally the King's Army marched for London. Feversham, in company with Churchill and the Duke of Grafton, went in advance of them to London for their rewards. Retribution for the wretched rebels was far from ended, however, for there was yet to come the Bloody Assize.

Orders came for Monmouth to be escorted to London. Although his hands were tied behind his back, he refused help in mounting his horse, but sprang to the saddle with something of his old élan, and joined by Lord Grey and Hollyday, left **Ringwood**, escorted by Lumley, Portman, and a large guard of regular troops and Militia, under orders, it is said, to stab him if there should be an attempt at rescue. Passing through **Romsey**, they arrived at **Winchester**, and spent the night at **Farnham Castle**, the home of Bishop Mews. They proceeded through Guildford, where they stayed in the tower of Archbishop Abbot's Hospital, and finally they reached **Vauxhall** where, Macaulay says, 'a regiment commanded by George Legge, Lord Dartmouth, was in readiness to receive the prisoners. They were put on board a state barge and carried down the river to Whitehall Stairs. The demeanour of both Monmouth and Lord Grey filled all observers with surprise. Monmouth was altogether unnerved. Grey was not only calm, but cheerful, talked pleasantly of horses, dogs and field sports, and even made jocose allusions to the perilous situation in which he stood.'

An audience was granted by the King, and Monmouth, his arms bound behind him by a silken cord, was ushered into the Royal presence. Macaulay wrote, 'Then Monmouth threw himself on the ground and crawled to the King's feet. He wept. He tried to embrace his uncle's knees with his pinioned arms. He begged for his life, only life at any price. He owned he had been guilty of a great crime, but tried to throw the blame on others... The unhappy man adjured James to show mercy.' James replied that he was sorry for the misery which he had brought on himself, 'but that the case was not one for lenity.' As to the Declaration, Monmouth said that he had not written it, but signed it without looking at it. It was all the work of Ferguson. "Do you expect me to believe," said James contemptuously, "that you set your hand to a paper of such moment without knowing what it contained?" Macaulay states that Monmouth, the Champion of the Protestant Religion, hinted that 'he was inclined to be reconciled to the Church of Rome.' The King eagerly offered him spiritual assistance – but not pardon. "Is there then no hope?" asked Monmouth. James turned away in silence. Then Monmouth strove to rally courage, rose from his knees, and retired with a firmness of courage which he had not shown since his overthrow.' "Poor Monmouth," James was heard to say, "He was always easy to be imposed upon."

Grey was the next to have an audience. He behaved with fortitude, made no excuses, 'and did not stoop to ask his life.' Both men returned to the Tower.

Tuesday, 14th July.

Since the Bill of Attainder recently passed by Parliament took the place of a trial, Monmouth was told by Bishop Turner of Ely and Bishop Ken of Bath and Wells that he would be executed the next day, July 15th, for high treason in levying war against the King. Although he asked for the execution to be delayed, his request was rejected. He signed a document stating that the title of 'King' had been forced upon him, and he declared that King Charles II had told him that he was never married to his mother, and said that he hoped that his children would not suffer 'on this account.' His Duchess was, by the Royal command, sent to see him. The meeting was frigid. Sbe told him that she had 'never troubled him but on two points – to complain about women, and his breach of duty towards the late King.' On the morning of his execution his wife brought their three children to say farewell to their father, and he 'bade his sons learn obedience to their King by his unhappy example.' The Duchess was visibly moved.

Dr. Tenison, Vicar of St Martin's in the Fields, whom Monmouth had requested to prepare him for his execution, urged him to repent of the sin of living with Henrietta, Lady Wentworth, but he refused to admit the sin. He impressed all by his devotion to prayer on the day before the execution.

Monmouth's Execution

The next day, Wednesday 15th July, James Scott, Duke of Monmouth, composed himself, and calmly asked his spiritual advisers, the Lords Bishops of Ely and of Bath and Wells, together with Doctors Tenison and Hooper, to attend him, 'but they told him in their judgement, he was about to die in a perilous state of mind, and that, if they attended him, it would be their duty to exhort him to the last.' He 'saluted' the guards with a smile as he passed, and with a firm tread mounted the draped scaffold.

Tower Hill was thronged to the chimney pots with people, the silence broken by sighs and weeping as the tall, slender, grey-clad figure addressed them. "I shall say but little," he began. "I come here not to speak but to die. I die a Protestant of the Church of England." The Bishops interrupted him, and told him that unless he acknowledged his sins he was no member of their Church. He went on to speak of Henrietta. She was, he said, a lady of virtue and honour, and far from deserving the unkind censure she lay under on his account. At this point he drew a ring from his finger and asked a bystander to give it to the Lady Henrietta. The Bishops continued their exhortations, and so 'discharged what, in their view, was a sacred duty.' When he was reminded of the 'ruin which he had brought on his brave and loving followers, of the blood which had been shed, of the souls which had been sent unprepared to the Great Account, he was touched, and said in a softened voice, "I do own that. I am sorry that it ever happened."

The Bishops continued to press him, and asked him to pray for the King, and to recommend his wife and his children to His Majesty's favour. He turned and said, "What harm have they done? Do it if your please; I pray for him and for all men." The Clergy began the prayers and responses, 'O Lord show Thy mercy upon us...' and were repeating them again when Monmouth interrupted with "Amen". They adjured him to speak a few words to the people on the duty of obedience to the Government. "I will make no speeches," he exclaimed. "I come to die." "Only ten words, my Lord," they said. Monmouth turned away, called to his servant, and put a toothpick case into his hand. "Give it," he said, "to that person to whom you are to deliver the other things." He turned to John Ketch, the executioner, 'a wretch who had butchered many brave and noble victims.' "Here are six guineas for you," said the Duke. "Do not hack me as you did my Lord Russell. I have heard you struck him three or four times." To his servant he said, "Here, take these remaining guineas, and give them to him if he does his work well." The executioner replied, "I hope I shall," to which Monmouth retorted, "If you strike me twice I cannot promise you not to stir."

As he prepared for the block the fifty-first Psalm was read, "Deliver me from bloodguiltiness, O God..." He lay down, and raising himself on his elbow said, "Prithee, let me feel the axe." He did so, and remarked, "I fear it is not sharp enough," "It is sharp enough and heavy enough," was the reply. He prayed again, then, unbound and without blindfold, he lay down again and gave the signal. Dr. Hooper turned away.

The axe fell, and merely gashed Monmouth's neck. He heaved himself up and looked reproachfully at the executioner. Held down by two or three men, he lowered his head once more. The second strike failed, and the next. Macaulay wrote, 'Ketch flung down the axe with a curse. "I cannot do it," he said, "My heart fails me." "Take up the axe, man!" cried the Sheriff. "Fling him over the rails!" roared the mob. At length the axe was taken up again. Two more blows extinguished the last remains of life; but a knife was used to separate the head from the shoulders. The crowd wrought up to such an ecstasy of rage that the executioner was in danger of being torn to pieces, and was conveyed away under a strong guard.'

Monmouth was regarded by many as a martyr who died for the Protestant Religion, and handkerchiefs were dipped in his blood and carried away as relics. His remains were placed in a coffin covered in black velvet, and a hearse drawn by six horses with funeral trappings took it back into the Tower, where the head was sewn on to the body. The corpse was privately laid under the communion table of St. Peter's Chapel in the Tower.

Lady Henrietta Wentworth died, of a broken heart it is said, in April 1686. Three years after Monmouth's death Anna, Duchess of Buccleuch, married Charles, Lord Cornwallis.

King James was not ungrateful to the man who had led those who put down the rebellion, and Feversham was made 'a Knight of the Garter and Captain of the first and most lucrative troop of Life Guards; but Court and City laughed at his military exploits, and the wit of Buckingham gave forth its last feeble flash at the expense of the general who had won a battle in bed.'

Meanwhile Col. Percy Kirke, left in command at **Bridgwater** by Feversham, continued his ruthless reign of terror. Kirke's Lambs went on with the carnage, although the Bishop of Wells spared 'neither expense nor pains in soothing the truly wretched side of the accumulating prisoners in Wells.' It was said that the Bishop warned Feversham after captured rebels had been hanged along the roadside. "My Lord," he said, "you do not know what you do. This is murder in the law... Now the Battle is over, these Rogues must be tried before they can be put to death." Kirke was not only cruel, but corrupt. For thirty or forty pounds he sold 'safe conduct,' by which the purchaser was permitted to pass without molestation to reach a seaport and escape to a foreign country. Great execution was done in **Taunton**.

Kirke was also susceptible to a pretty woman. There was a tradition that the Vestal Virgins of ancient Rome had the privilege of begging the life of any condemned man they might meet on his way to execution. The relatives of one of Kirke's prisoners thought to attempt something of this sort, and they persuaded Mrs.Elizabeth Rowe, 'a lady of great and most amiable character, for which she was deservedly famous all over the West,' to go, dressed in white, to Colonel Kirke and beg his life. This she did, and the ploy succeeded, for Kirke turned to one of his officers, Lieutenant Bush, and bade him, "Go and tell the executioner to cut him free." Bush, a stupid man, had not heard the name of the fortunate prisoner, and without waiting to ask, went to the executioner and said, "You must cut him free." "Cut him free! Which 'him', for there are twenty?" replied the executioner. The young man concerned was busy praying, unaware of this exchange, but another prisoner who had been attending to the proceedings, and was quick of wit, told Bush that he was the one. Bush pointed him out to the executioner, who cut his bonds, and the wily opportunist jumped out of the cart and ran away. The man who should have been reprieved was hanged, the truth being discovered too late.

Whilst the executioner was performing his horrible task, 'Kirke with his characteristic barbarity commanded the fifes to play, the trumpets to sound and the drums to beat, that the music might drown the cries of the dying victims. The bodies of these unfortunate men were, by his order, immediately stripped, their breasts cleft asunder, and their hearts, while warm, separately flung into a large fire; and as each was cast in, a great shout was raised, the executioner saying, "There goes the heart of a traitor!" Their quarters were boiled in pitch, and hung up at all crossways and public parts of the town and neighbourhood.'

A few days after Kirke's arrival in Taunton he wrote to London to ask what he should do with those rebels then in custody. Lord Sunderland informed him on 14th July that he was to secure them in some prison or other safe place until their trial at the Assize. Kirke turned to selling pardons to wealthier men who could meet his demands. He wrote again to London on 22nd July for three such pardons, and on 25th July Lord Sunderland replied, "His Majesty does not think fit to do anything of that kind; all such as they shall be tried before my Lord Chief Justice and other Judges appointed to the Western Circuit; after which I doubt not but, upon your application, His Majesty will be ready to gratify you in any reasonable request of this nature, wherein I shall be glad to give you my best assistance.' Kirke allowed some of his men to lodge 'at free quarters,' which was a hardship to the people, and the Mayor of Bridgwater complained to the Secretary of State. The Government was dissatisfied with Kirke on account both of his barbarity and the 'interested lenity which he had shown to rich delinquents,' and he was soon recalled from the West Country.

As a prelude to the Assize, orders were sent to the Constables of all the parishes in the Hundreds of Dorset, Devon and Somerset to produce lists of all those suspected of being involved in the rebellion, those who were away from their homes at the time, and those who had provided the rebels with food, horses, shelter or other assistance. These rolls formed the basis of the evidence which the Lord Chief Justice was to use to convict and sentence the prisoners, and to be a powerful deterrent to would-be malcontents and traitors.

Judge Jeffreys, from a portrait in Judge Jeffreys' Restaurant, Dorchester, Dorset.

THE "BLOODY ASSIZE"

For the bloody work of judicial retribution to be wreaked on the wretched rebels King James chose well. George, Lord Jeffreys, Lord Chief Justice of England, Baron of Wem, a man noted for his brutality and lack of mercy, headed the Circuit of Judges. His four colleagues were The Honourable William Montague, Lord Chief Baron of His Majesty's Court of Exchequer, with Sir Robert Wright, a Baron of the same Court; Sir Creswell Levinz, a Justice of the Court of Common Pleas; and Sir Francis Wythens, Justice of the Court of Queen's Bench. Chief Prosecutor was Sir Henry Pollexfen, a Whig. The normal Summer Assizes had had to be adjourned due to the rebellion, and this build-up of cases had to be dealt with before attention could be turned to the hundreds of rebels locked up in the foetid gaols of the West Country.

The Trial of Lady Alice Lisle

Tuesday, 25th August.
    The Lord Chief Justice opened the first Court of the Assize at **Winchester**. Although the men of Hampshire had not been actively involved in the rebellion, many rebels had escaped to that county.
    After Sedgemoor, two of the rebels, John Hicks, a non-conformist minister, and Richard Nelthorpe, outlawed for being implicated in the Rye House Plot, had escaped together to **Warminster** and taken refuge with James Dunne, a baker, who managed to keep them concealed from the Militia patrolling that area. They slept by day and hid in the countryside at night. Seeking a more secure haven, Hicks wrote to Lady Alice Lisle, an old acquaintance of his, asking her to give them lodgings. Lady Lisle, who had been in London during the rebellion, had returned after Monmouth's execution to her home, **Moyles Court** at **Ellingham** on the Avon between **Ringwood** and **Fordingbridge.**
    Dunne the baker was entrusted with the letter, and taking an unobtrusive route through **Longbridge Deverill**, he became lost at **Chilmark**. He called at the cottage of a labourer, John Barter, and begged him to guide him to Ellingham. Barter led him through **Fovant** and **Broad Chalke** to Fordingbridge, and along the Avon to Moyles Court, where Goodman Carpenter, Lady Lisle's bailiff, took Dunne to his mistress. She read the letter, and questioned Dunne about the two men who sought lodgings with her, but Dunne did not reveal that they were rebel fugitives. He may have been too anxious to get them out of

Moyles Court, Ellingham, the home in 1685 of Lady Alice Lisle.

his house to be wholly truthful. Seeing the guide Barter in the kitchen, she joked with Dunne; Barter, who was of a suspicious nature, later asked Dunne what the laughter was about, and he said that she had asked 'if he knew anything of the 'concern'.' Dunne and Barter left together, and on their way Barter learned that two wealthy men were coming to stay at Moyles Court the following Tuesday night, July 28th. The two men parted, and Dunne made his way back to Warminster.

Lady Alice Lisle was the widow of John Lisle, who had been one of Cromwell's new Peers, and a judge at the sentencing of Charles I. At the Restoration he had fled the country, and had died by assassination in 1664. He had had enemies at home, too. In 1655 he had sentenced to death for treason the father of Colonel Penruddock, a Tory magistrate of nearby **Compton Chamberlayne**. Lady Lisle herself, however, was 'esteemed by the Tory gentlemen of her county.'

John Barter was suspicious of Dunne's 'two wealthy men.' Instead of returning home, he made his way to Compton Chamberlayne and told Colonel Penruddock his tale.

Hicks and Nelthorpe, with Dunne as their guide, duly arrived at Moyles Court, and Lady Lisle gave them hospitality and 'showed them where they might take their rest,' but when she discovered from Hicks the true nature of their plight, 'she instantly despatched her principal servant to a Justice of the Peace with information concerning them, but gave special orders that they might be suffered to escape.'

She was too late. By the next morning the mansion was surrounded by soldiers, and Colonel Penruddock was hammering on the door. Lady Lisle protested that there were no fugitives in the house, but a search was made. Hicks and Dunne were discovered in the Malt House, and Nelthorpe was either up a chimney or close by one. All, including

Lady Lisle, were made prisoner.

On the 27th August at Winchester Castle, the Lord Chief Justice determined to set the scene for all the subsequent trials. He was to try Dame Alice Lisle, an elderly widow, for treason. Hers was the only trial on this particular charge to be held in Hampshire at this time, and Jeffreys was set to exact punishment of the highest order in the case of this elderly lady, who was one of very few of her class to be brought to trial. She was an unfortunate victim of Jeffrey's ruthless determination to create the severest possible atmosphere for the subsequent progress of the Assize, and to strike fear and despair in the hearts of all his victims to come. She was in no sense a rebel, and indeed at the time neither Hicks nor Nelthorpe had been brought to trial, let alone convicted, of treason or rebellion.

The Court was hung in scarlet, and the five Judges sat in their scarlet robes and heavy periwigs, the Baron of Wem on his throne in the centre. The frail, elderly figure stood before them, so deaf that a man was appointed to stand beside her to repeat what was said. A jury of 'men of standing' was sworn in, and the trial began.

The witnesses who were called were the men who had been taken prisoner by the rebels at the attack at Keynsham on June 25th. Monmouth had sent Hicks and his Chaplain Ferguson to see how the prisoners were faring in the stables of Sir Thomas Bridges, and their food had been improved on Hick's orders. They swore that it was the same man who had visited them. Dunne was called, and Pollexfen said that as this was a very unwilling witness he hoped that the Court would examine him with severity. Jeffreys needed no prompting, and literally put the fear of God into Dunne before he began to give evidence, telling him 'not to tempt God to strike him into the bottomless lake of Hell.'

Dunne told a story by which he hoped both to clear himself of treason and to give no damaging evidence against Lady Lisle, but under Jeffrey's merciless questioning he broke down, repeating the Judge's questions in a stupid manner, for he was, he said, 'quite cluttered out of his senses.' "O how hard the truth is," said Jeffreys, "to come out of a lying Presbyterian knave!" Then, as Dunne stammered a few more words, "Was there ever such a villain on the face of the earth? Dost thou believe there is a God? Dost thou believe in Hell fire? Of all the witnesses I ever met with I never saw thy fellow." Dunne faltered, "I cannot tell what to say, my Lord." The Judge, angrily, with obscene language, replied, "Was there ever such an impudent rascal? Hold a candle to him that we may see his brazen face. You, Gentlemen, that are of counsel for the Crown, see that information for perjury be prepared against this fellow."

The witness was dismissed. Lady Alice Lisle, who had pleaded 'Not guilty', was called for questioning. She said that she had known that Hicks was in trouble when she agreed to shelter him, but she did not know, and had no suspicion, of his involvement in the rebellion. She had thought that he was a non-conformist priest who had been in danger for preaching. The Lord Chief Justice stormed "There is not one of these lying, snivelling, canting Presbyterians but one way or another had a hand in the rebellion. Show me a Presbyterian and I'll show thee a lying knave!" Alice Lisle told the Court that her son, on her advice, had taken up arms against the rebels, and that she had condemned the rising of Monmouth.

In his summing up Jeffreys reminded the jury that the prisoner's husband had borne a part in the death of Charles I, (which was not proved, and was in any case totally irrelevant). For an hour he declaimed against the Whigs and Dissenters, and the jurymen were warned to disregard the prisoner's age and sex when considering their verdict.

They deliberated long over their decision, and growing impatient, the Judge sent for them to return instantly, 'or he would adjourn the Court and lock them up for the night.' They questioned whether the charge could be made, because Hicks was still at Wells awaiting trial. They were not clear whether the prisoner knew that Hicks was in the rebel army or not, a point that could have made the difference between the verdict of 'Guilty' or 'Not guilty.' Jeffreys mis-directed the jury. Hicks, he said, might have been wounded, and died at the House, in which case he could never have been convicted, but still he would have been a rebel, having already confessed to having been at Sedgemoor. Because of this, the subsequent conviction of Alice Lisle was annulled after the Revolution of 1688. The Judge then, Sir Matthew Hale, stated that the 'harbouring' charge could not in future be pressed until 'the Principal is convicted.'

However, this legal nicety of the future was of little help to the unfortunate prisoner. Jeffreys raged at the jury, and they reluctantly returned a verdict of 'Guilty'. The Lord Chief Justice was satisfied, and merely added, "If I had been among you, and she had been my own mother, I should have found her Guilty!"

The sentence was that she be burned alive, and the Sheriff was ordered to prepare for her execution that afternoon. Fearful that she might be reprieved, Jeffreys said, "We that are the Judges shall stay in town an hour or two. You," he said to Alice Lisle, "shall have pen, ink and paper brought to you, and if in the meantime you employ that pen, ink and paper well this hour or two, well (you understand what I mean), it may be you may hear further from us in deferring the execution." This could have been a hint for revealing the names of other rebels, or for a bribe. She merely asked that she should be beheaded instead of the burning.

The Clergy of Winchester Cathedral protested vehemently at this barbarous treatment of Alice Lisle. The Lord Chief Justice delayed the execution for five days, and her friends pleaded with the King to show her mercy. Feversham went to him and begged the life of Lady Lisle, but he replied that he had promised Jeffreys not to pardon her, and on Wednesday 2nd September she was beheaded in Winchester Market Place, saying, "I forgive all persons that have done me wrong, and I desire that God will do so likewise." Her remains were taken by her daughters to Ellingham Church.

This was, by any standard, an unjust conviction because of the sequence of the Lisle – Hicks trials, but it was not unfounded on the evidence. It was regarded as being politically the most distasteful event in the reign of James II. He had taken revenge on a Regicide's aged widow, and alienated many of his supporters, so contributing to his final removal from the throne in favour of William of Orange.

Judge Jeffreys went on to **Salisbury** to open the Assize there, but the Judges found little to do beyond sentencing a few to be fined or whipped for uttering 'seditious words'. One young man, Stephen Moore, who had declared that he wouldn't go to Church until Monmouth was King was, with grim humour, sentenced to be whipped from outside the city to his parish church, and then to make 'an uncomfortable pilgimage' to Salisbury Cathedral.

The dreaded Judiciary progressed to **Dorchester**, the County Town of Dorset, and well into rebel country. Jeffreys opened the Commission on Thursday, 3rd September, and the following day he attended Divine Service at St Peter's Church, during which, according to Macaulay, 'it was rumoured that when the clergyman who preached the Assize sermon inforced the duty of Mercy, the ferocious mouth of the Judge was distorted by an ominous grin. These things made men augur ill of what was to follow.' Loyal supporters of birth and position were there from Dorset, Somerset and Devon.

Lady Lisle's tombstone in Ellingham churchyard.

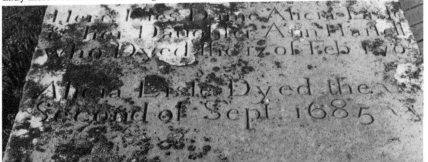

The Dorchester Assize

The Court was held, it is believed, in what is known as the Oak Room in the Antelope Hotel in **Dorchester**, and the Chief Justice again ordered the room to be hung in scarlet. The 'judicial massacre' began.

Over three hundred prisoners were to be tried, and it was obvious that each of this vast number could not expect a fair trial in the short time available for the Dorchester Assize. Hundreds more rebels awaited trial throughout the West Country, and the business was to be carried out within the space of one month. Jeffrey's patience and temper were by no means improved by the excruciatingly painful malady from which he was then suffering – the disease of 'the stone' – and to speed matters he 'let it be understood that the only chance of obtaining pardon or respite was to plead guilty.' By pleading 'not guilty', prisoners upon conviction could be certain of execution. By pleading 'guilty' there was a reasonable chance instead of the wretched fate of transportation.

Jeffreys charged his jury to find out others, besides the rebels, who were 'Abettors, Aiders or Assisters to the late Duke of Monmouth,' and said with the utmost clarity that he was there to 'breathe death like a destroying angel and to sanguine his very ermins in blood.' The first thirty-four rebels went before him and pleaded 'not guilty'. Twenty-nine of these were convicted and sentenced to be hanged on the following Monday; one, Saunders, was acquitted for lack of evidence; and the remainder changed their plea to 'guilty', and were sentenced to execution. John Ketch was one of the two men brought from London to carry out the executions. He had beheaded Monmouth, and was often associated with Jeffreys in the lampoons of the day. One said, 'While Jeffreys on the bench, Ketch on the gibbet sits.' The two executioners Ketch and Paxha Rose complained that they could not complete so many hangings in one day, and in the event thirteen rebels died on Monday and the remainder followed soon after.

One of the thirteen was Thomas Smith of **Chardstock**, who had been compelled to hand over some Militia money to a party of the Duke's men. He told his story to the jury, observing at the same time that 'little credit ought to be given to the evidence, as they were the same who had before witnessed against his neighbour Mr. Bragg.' Upon this the Judge put himself in violent passion, saying, "Thou villain! Methinks I see thee already with a halter about thy neck! Thou impudent rebel, to challenge the king's evidence!" Being found guilty, he was, on the special orders of the Judge, the first man to be executed.

St. Peter's Church, Dorchester, Dorset, where the Assize Sermon was preached in the 4th September, 1685. The head of an executed rebel was later displayed here on a spike.

Judge Jeffreys' Restaurant, Dorchester, Dorset, reputed to have been the Judge's lodging during the Bloody Assize at Dorchester in September 1685.

The Antelope Hotel, Dorchester, Dorset, where, it is believed, the Assize was held.

The Oak Room in the Antelope Hotel, Dorchester, where the Assize is thought to have taken place.

Some deaths are recorded of men who were completely innocent. Mr. Bragg, an attorney-at-law of **Sadborow, Thorncombe** near Chard, was returning home and met a party of Monmouth's cavalry. They forced him to show them the way to the house of a Roman Catholic, where they searched for arms. They also seized his horse, and had to walk home to Sadborow. He was rapidly convicted, and executed on the Monday. Jeffreys had often bragged that 'if a lawyer or a parson came under his inspection they should not escape.'

Christopher Battiscombe, a young lawyer who lived near **Lyme Regis**, was also brought to trial. He is reported to have been invited several times to the Judge's lodgings, where he offered him a pardon if he would impeach others, but this he refused to do. His fiancée knelt to the Judge and begged for his life, but the cruel insulting reply was 'that he could only spare her part of him; but as he knew what she wanted it should be that part which she liked best, and he would give orders to the sheriff accordingly.' He was sent to be hanged at Lyme Regis.

Another prisoner, Captain Madders, or Mardens, a Constable of **Crewkerne**, who had quickly sent a report of the Duke's landing to the King, then later accepted command of a company in the Duke's service, was captured at Sedgemoor. He would probably have been pardoned, but one of the witnesses overdid it by describing him as a good Protestant. "Oho!" said Jeffreys, "He is a Presbyterian! I can smell them at forty miles. He shall be hanged." He was, at Lyme Regis. Richard Hollyday was accused of of 'conducting the Lord Grey from **Gillingham** to **Ringwood** after the fight at Weston.' He was found guilty, and sentenced to be fined and whipped. John Kidd, the gamekeeper from **Longleat**, who served Monmouth well and was knighted by him, was sent for execution at **Lyme**.

John Tuchins, alias Thomas Pills, was sentenced for what might be called today 'spreading alarm and despondency'. He had declared that Argyll's army was near London, that Hampshire supported Monmouth, and that he had seen his forces near **Christchurch**. He was sentenced to be whipped in the market towns of the county, and to be imprisoned for seven years. In fact, he was released the next year.

Jeffreys wrote to Earl Sunderland on the Saturday, 5th September, "I this day have begun with the trial of the Rebels at **Dorchester**, and have despatched 98," and, in the same sentence, "but am at this time so tortured with the stone that I must beg your Lordship's intercession to His Majesty for the incoherence of what I have adventured to give His Majesty the trouble of and that I may give myself so much ease by your Lordship's favour as to make use of my servant's pen to give a relation of what has happened since I came here."

The sentence for high treason was hanging, drawing and quartering. At the Dorchester Assize nearly three hundred men were sentenced to this fate, but in practice many of those had their sentence commuted to transportation, and reports state that seventy-four were executed, one hundred and seventy five transported and twenty nine were pardoned. There was a brisk business in the sale of pardons. Those executed in Dorset were hung in the main towns in an area stretching from **Poole** to **Lyme Regis**, but not inland at Blandford and Shaftesbury.

On the day before the executions at Lyme Regis were to take place, which was September 12th, the Mayor of Lyme entertained the Judges lavishly on their way to Exeter. In the Philpot Museum in Lyme Regis is an account for entertaining Judge Jeffreys, including 'Wine and Sturgeon,' and 'Powder' needed to fire a salvo of honour for Jeffreys and his fellow Judges on the Commission when they entered the town. The next day a sledge was prepared to take the condemned men on their arrival down to the place of execution, a spot near to where Monmouth had originally landed. Horses were hitched to the sledge, but they refused to move, and this was regarded as 'an Act of God, a miracle'. Other horses were brought, but now the sledge broke on the rough cobbles, and so the prisoners were made to walk. There was the elderly Sampson Larke, once the Baptist minister. His flock were broken-hearted. His last speech to the people was brusquely interrupted by the guard, who told him that there was so much work to do that they could not spare him the time to finish. Dr. Temple of Nottingham was there. He had gone to Holland to gain more experience of medicine, where he had met the Duke, who employed him as a physician and surgeon. He had no idea that Monmouth was planning to invade England until he had been at sea for some time, but

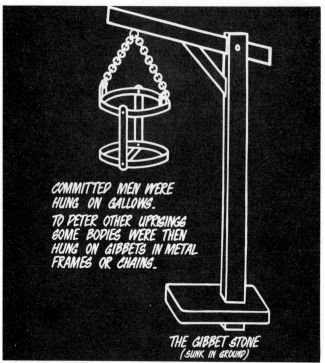

COMMITTED MEN WERE
HUNG ON GALLOWS.

TO DETER OTHER UPRISINGS
SOME BODIES WERE THEN
HUNG ON GIBBETS IN METAL
FRAMES OR CHAINS.

THE GIBBET STONE
(SUNK IN GROUND)

The Swanage Gibbet Stone at the Tithe Barn, Swanage, Dorset. Some of the bodies of executed rebels were hung on gibbets in iron frames or chains.

this did not help him at his trial, and he 'therefore resigned himself to his fate with becoming fortitude.' William Hewling, a much admired young Lieutenant of Foot, a man of 'very sweet and obliging temper,' was executed. His body continued to hang until the next day. It was not quartered, but taken down with quiet ceremony, and no one prevented the young women of Lyme Regis as, braving the authorities and the wrath of the terrible Jeffreys, and accompanied by some two hundred people, they bore the body of the handsome young man to a grave in Lyme churchyard.

The Philpot Museum at Lyme holds 'the Hewling Manuscript, 1685-90.' This was a plea to Judge Jeffreys for mercy, written by Hannah Hewling, the sister of Benjamin and William Hewling, who had supported Monmouth. Benjamin was hanged at Taunton. Hannah is said to have 'supplicated the Judge's mercy in favour of her brother (William), offering one hundred pounds but for two days' respite, and laying hold on one of the wheels of his coach, seemingly to stay with it until her request was granted. Jeffreys, however, regardless of her tears, ordered the coachman to cut her hands with his whip.'

The Exeter Assize

Judge Jeffreys arrived in Exeter. He opened the Assize with his usual warning that an unsuccessful plea of 'not guilty' would be followed by a quick execution after the verdict. In spite of this, two men, John Foweracres (or Fouracres) and Robert Drowser pleaded 'not guilty'. Fouracres failed to convince the jury of his inocence, and the Judge sentenced him to be executed immediately. Drowser, however, was reprieved. All the other prisoners pleaded 'guilty'. 'Twenty one were sentenced and one was reprieved. Thirteen were executed and their heads and quarters distributed around the country. Thirteen were fined and whipped for speaking seditious words. The Assistant Deputy Sheriff of Devon directed that the quarters and heads of the rebels were to be sent to **Honiton, Axminster, Colyton, Ottery, Crediton, Bideford, Barnstaple, Torrington, Tiverton, Plymouth, Dartmouth** and **Totnes.**

The prisoners were generally well looked after by unknown benefactors. All kinds of provisions were sent to them, and they had the attention of a nurse or doctor if needed.

An interesting feature of this Assize was the publishing of three hundred and forty-two names of those people still at large when the session ended. These were men who had successfully hidden from the military and civil authorities, some even living in copses and haystacks, and being cared for by their friends.

The local magistrates and people of Devon were sickened and shocked by the barbarity of the authorities, and by seeing the blood, and the severed flesh of the victims hanging by the roadside, and a storm of protest arose as the Judge left Exeter.

The Taunton Assize

Thursday, 17th September.

As the Judges travelled from Exeter to Taunton through the villages and towns of Somerset it seemed that every crossroad, every market place and every village green bore its grisly quota of corpses hanging in irons, or heads and quarters on poles. The air was foul with the stench from the miserable remains, but Macaulay wrote, 'The Chief Justice was all himself. His spirits rose higher and higher as the work went on. He laughed, shouted, joked and swore in such a way that many thought him drunk from morning to night. But in him it was not easy to distinguish the madness produced by evil passions from the madness produced by brandy.'

Here, the wretched prisoners were confined in crowded gaols, some suffering from typhoid and smallpox, and the diseases spread to the surrounding areas. There were five hundred in the hot and sweltering gaols of **Taunton.**

On a wall at the entrance to the Tudor Tavern in Taunton is an old board on which is written:

> 'Ye Musings of Ye Judge Jeffries
> Bloody Judge Indeed!
>
> The love of Fairplay and Justice is in the very Marrow of my Bones. What could be fairer than my command at ye start of each Case – Bring in ye next prisoner and let us see his rascally face – It is a warning to ye Villains to be on their Best behaviour and not to waste ye Court's time by pleading innocence.'

In the Great Hall of Taunton Castle on Friday, September 18th the customary scene was set, the five judges sitting in their scarlet robes and heavy wigs, with the Lord Chief Justice Baron Jeffreys of Wem enthroned in the centre. The Gaol Delivery numbered five hundred and fourteen prisoners. Four of them pleaded 'not guilty', and they, being convicted, were sentenced to execution on the following Monday at Taunton. The remainder were tried in two days. Hundreds pleaded 'guilty', and were sentenced for High Treason.

Lord Staywell of **Somerton**, a Tory Peer, was among those sickened by Jeffreys' sadistic brutality, and he refused to entertain him during the Taunton Assize. In return for this slight, Jeffreys ordered the bodies of Colonel Bovet and another executed rebel to be suspended in chains outside his park gate.

John Churchill is said to have tried to help Hannah Hewling in her petition to save her brother Benjamin, their younger brother having been condemned at **Dorchester**, but when Churchill saw her again about the petition he told her the quest was hopeless, and putting his hand on the mantelpiece he said, "The King's heart is as incapable of feeling compassion as that marble." It cost Hannah a thousand pounds to buy the right to convey her brother's remains to the Church of St Mary Magdalen at **Taunton.**

The sequel to the pretty tale of the *Maids of Taunton* and their parade before Monmouth was a sad story. Miss Blake died of smallpox in Dorchester Gaol. Susannah Musgrave, the other school-mistress and all the children were hauled before the Court, 'for they were part of the loot of the campaign,' and a ransom had to be paid for them by their parents. Jeffreys railed at one little girl in the Great Hall with his usual savagery and ordered the jailer to take her to prison. It is said that this so frightened the child that, crying, she drew her hood over her face and in a few hours died of fright. All the *Maids of Taunton* were given by the King as a 'Christmas Box' to the Queen and the Maids of Honour. At Taunton, as at Dorchester, hundreds of convicts were handed over to Courtiers, including 'to the Queen's order one hundred. Many pardons were trafficked in and sold, according to the wealth of the suitor, for sums ranging from ten pounds to fourteen thousand guineas.'

Jeffreys finished his work in Taunton in three days. One hundred and forty six prisoners were sentenced to execution, of whom two were reprieved, at least two hundred and eighty four were transported, and thirty two were pardoned. 'By filing one of the bars of their window in the prison cell, three prisoners escaped down a rope, having left their shackles behind uncut and unbroken.'

A copy of a warrant from Edward Hobbs, High Sheriff of Somerset to the officers of Bath throws some light on the 'whole form and apparatus required to execute the sentences passed upon the prisoners.'

"Whereas I have received a warrant under the hand and seal of the Right Honourable the Lord Jeffreys for the executing of several Rebels within your said City. These are to will and require you immediately on sight hereof to erect a Gallows in the most public place of your said City to hang the said Traitors on, and that you provide halters to hang them with, a sufficient number of faggots to burn the bowls of fower (four?) Traitors, and a furnace or cauldron to boil their heads and quarters and salt to boil herewith, half a Bushell to each Traitor, and tar to tar them with, and sufficient number of spears and poles to fix and place their heads and quarters: and that you warn the owners of four Oxen to be ready with the dray and wain, and the said four Oxen, at a time hereafter mentioned for execution, and you yourselves, together with a guard of forty able men at least, to be present on Wednesday morning next by eight of the clock, to be aiding and assisting to me or my deputie to see the said rebels executed...

Given this day under my Seal of Office
this 16th Day of November
Jacobi Secundi 1685

You are also to provide an axe and a cleaver for the quartering the said Rebels."

He also laid down the distribution of heads and quarters. After twelve had been executed near or on Greenhill at Weymouth he directed that the members be distributed to **Upwey, Sutton Poyntz, Osmington, Preston Weeks, Winfrith, Broadmayne, Radipole, Winterborne St Martin, Puddletown** and **Bincombe**. In **Weymouth** they were to be put at Grand Pier, Town's End, near Windmill, Town Hall, or the Bridge, and Melcombe Town Hall. The dismembered bodies were in fact to stay until the King made a tour of the West Country in the Summer of 1686.

One unpopular character was Tom Boilman, so named because of his occupation at this time, which also included tarring the remains. Ploughing one day near **North Petherton**, he sheltered under an oak tree from a violent thunderstorm. He was struck dead, by what was generally adjudged to be a Heaven-directed flash of lightning. A farmer named Raphael of Grendon Farm near Lidgate, in **Combpyne** parish, provided gorse faggots for burning entrails. He was named Burnman, and reviled by the people, and it is said that 'he and his horses visibly pined away.'

The Wells Assize

Tuesday, 22nd September.

The Market Hall at **Wells** was the scene of the end of the Bloody Assize. There were five hundred and forty two prisoners, of whom ninety nine were sentenced to execution, although one, Roger Hoare, was reprieved. The rest were transported. Among those sentenced at Wells was Charles Speke, son of George Speke of **Whitelackington**, who had shaken hands with Monmouth as he passed through Ilminster. The Major of the 1st Regiment of Guards asked Jeffreys whether any favour would be shown him; he replied, 'No. His family owes a life. He shall die for his brother, who is guilty of being in the action, but has escaped.' His execution took place at Ilminster, where he was hanged from a tree after praying for nearly an hour and singing a psalm, surrounded by the local inhabitants, who uttered the most heart-rending lamentations.

At the **Bristol** Assize the Court List was very slight, as there were no rebels to be tried.

SOME CONSEQUENCES

The Lord Chief Justice left behind a trail of cruelty, misery and despair in his punishment of the rebels, but he had performed as his master the King had wished and expected him to do. On his return to London the King, on 28th September, signified his entire approval of the conduct of the Assize by committing to his custody the Great Seal of England, with the title of Lord Chancellor, and five days later His Majesty publicly received all five of the Judges and thanked them for their services, thereby showing his support for all that they had done.

Why one man should be sentenced to death, another to transportation, and yet another should be pardoned was never clear, although the money that could be made from men transported or pardoned probably had a considerable bearing on the sentence chosen.

Eight hundred and forty men were sent for transportation, and in many cases they were as surely sentenced to death as if they had been ordered to be hanged, except that death was postponed. Their destination was the islands of the West Indies, where the grinding physical labour under hot sun, the living conditions of a white slave, and the prevalence of yellow fever ensured that few would survive the ten years of servitude to which they were condemned. These men were given to favoured courtiers on condition that they were sent to the West Indies, and they were valuable booty, being worth ten or fifteen pounds each on the slave market. Those who bought them did so either to sell them again at a profit, or to put them to work in their own plantations in the West Indies. Men who had been transported to Barbados were 'grinding at the mills, attending at the furnaces, and digging in that scorching island, being bought and sold still from one planter to another, or attached as horses or beasts for the debts of their masters, being whipped at whipping posts as rogues at their master's pleasure, and sleeping in sites worse than hogs in England.'

One in five of those tranported was, it is said, 'flung to the sharks before the end of the voyage.' The human cargoes were crammed into the holds of the small vessels, and given so little space that they could not all lie down at once without lying on top of each other. This, together with festering untreated wounds, disease, foetid conditions from the lack of fresh air, and the lack of any exercise on deck all contributed to the death of many of the prisoners in the wretched dungeons below decks. In one ship, of ninety nine convicts, twenty two died before reaching Jamaica, and this was one of the fastest voyages. On arrival at their destination the conditions under which they had travelled, together with scarce rations of coarse biscuit and foetid water had taken their toll. Near skeletons arrived, and dealers had to fatten them up before offering them for sale.

One of those transported was John Coad, a carpenter who was wounded at **Norton St. Philip**. His description of his experiences gave insight into the conditions of slavery in Jamaica. Held in the cloisters at **Wells** and awaiting execution, Coad managed to take the place of a prisoner in the queue of those to be transported, and under the name of John Haker he joined the men who marched from Wells to **Weymouth**. During this long march about thirty men escaped and one received a reprieve, whilst a further three escaped from **Sherborne** Gaol where they rested for two nights. Many were sick, and were thrown into carts. At Weymouth they eventually took ship for Jamaica in conditions described above. John Coad endured the lice and the sickness, and on arrival in Jamaica he, together with others of the prisoners who were relatively fit, was separated from the remainder, and they were sold in groups, or 'parcels,' of about six. As a skilled carpenter Coad was put to more congenial work than sweating in the fields of sugar cane, or stoking the sugar boilers, and he managed to stay alive and return home at the end of his sentence, landing at Plymouth on November 29th, 1690.

The Cloisters at Wells Cathedral.

A much more comfortable time was enjoyed by Azariah Pinney, son of John Pinney, once Non-conformist Minister of **Broadwindsor**. Azariah was listed with others as a rebel with the words 'being witness' by their names, which suggests that they turned King's Evidence. His wealthy father paid £65 to a factor named George Penne, and a further £5 for passage from **Bristol** in a pink, and he took with him provisions of brandy and cheese, and 'six gallons of sack.' Technically he was serving his sentence of transporation, but he was doing it in comfort, and he lived as a free man in the West Indies and made money there. Some say that traces of a Somerset accent may be detected in the native speech in Barbados even now.

By law a man guilty of treason forfeits all his property, and in the West Country after the Bloody Assize there were large numbers of desperate widows and orphans being hounded by Treasury agents who came to confiscate what remained of dead rebels' property. They were questioned on what had become of food, cider, geese, bacon, and even a truss of hay. It is recorded that the widow of Henry Watts, a smallholder of **Whitchurch Canonicorum**, was allowed a pittance to keep her from utter destitution.

Government agents of another kind were reaping rich pickings from the families of rebels of the more wealthy kind. Mr. Burd of **Beckington**, said to have proclaimed Monmouth King at the head of four thousand men, was taken into custody. The Bishop of Bath and Wells, good man that he was, managed to procure his discharge, but he was apprehended a second time and committed to prison by Lord Feversham. At his trial at **Wells** he was sentenced to be executed, but being turned over to the Pardon-monger he was able to purchase his life at the cost of four hundred pounds.

At a much higher level again, Jeffreys assiduously lined his pockets by dealing in pardons among some of the great Whig families. His greatest coup resulted from persuading the King to 'give' him Edmund Prideaux, of **Forde Abbey**. Two people of rank, one of them Lady Churchill, had applied to the King for Mr. Prideaux, but were told that 'the King had given him to Jeffreys,' which gave Jeffreys the right to set his own terms for the release of Prideaux. He settled for the enormous sum of £14,500, and was able to buy two fine estates and manors of Dalby on the Wold and Nether Broughton in Leicestershire from the Duke of Albermarle.

Major-General Lord John Churchill received as his reward the property of John Hucker, a **Taunton** serge-maker who was hanged at Taunton, and was given the colonelcy of the third troop of the horseguards on 1st August 1685.

Medals struck by command of James II after the defeat of Monmouth's rebellion.

Some of the more prominent supporters of Monmouth evaded the retribution which claimed so many. Lord Grey, Wade, Story, Jones and Goodenough all turned King's Evidence, and were spared. Wade was given a full pardon in October, and went back to his career at law, ending his days as Town Clerk of Bristol. The Reverend Ferguson, Monmouth's Chaplain, had escaped to Holland, where he probably plagued Skelton. Eventually he became a Roman Catholic. Monmouth's personal Chaplain, the Reverend Hook, also turned to the Roman faith.

Richard Nelthorpe was already beyond the law by reason of his connection with the Rye House Plot, and no trial was needed for him. He was executed by the gate at Grays Inn.

In the final count it is estimated that about seven percent of Monmouth's rebel army were either killed in battle or executed afterwards. The West Country lost something in the region of four thousand men of its working population. Over one thousand prisoners were either hanged or transported, and not until the General Pardon of March 1686 did hundreds more dare to re-appear.

As to the battle casualties, five hundred and eighty men of the Royalist army were killed during the rebellion, and one thousand eight hundred and ten of Monmouth's men died. How many men died of wounds on the two sides is not known, nor how many died of disease, or never returned from transportation.

Monmouth's rebellion was joined not only by religious fanatics fighting in the name of the Protestant Religion but also by simple people, poor people, people with a simple faith in their religion. Monmouth, with his youth, charm and warm personality appealed to the kindly folk of the West Country. They saw in him no tyrant, or Popish oppressor, and they flocked to his side. The rebels fought bravely at Sedgemoor, and died faithfully for their cause.

The final intolerance and brutality of the regime of King James II personified in Judge Jeffreys led eventually to the upsurge of revulsion by the people which swept James from the throne on 11th December 1688 after William of Orange had landed at **Torbay**.

James Scott, Duke of Monmouth, who bent easily to the persuasions of those who wished to use him, would in all probability not have been of sufficient firmness to be the right King for the country even had he been the legitimate son of Charles II. As Bishop Burnt wrote, "He was soft and gentle even to excess, and too easy to those who had credit with him. He was both sincere and good natured."

DIEV ET MON DROIT

QVONI OPENSI

Sutte pile

Flathōlmes Iland

hepholme Iland

Stert poynt

Botestall poynt

Porshut
Crokampill
Shire hampton
Porthburye
St George
Weston
Clyston
Walton parke
PORTBVRY
Lye
Clopton
Fayland
Walton HVND
Wraxhall
Wakestowre
Tykenham
Rounam passage Longasshto
Bedminster
Clouedon
Naylesey
Burton
Bisport
Kéne
Cheuelay
Part of Brockley
Blackwell
Barrow
Dundrey
HARTCLIFF &
Felton
CHI
Kingston Chewton Hund
Eaton
BED MINSTER
Winford
Bishop
Kingeswood Brodweldon
Chue slu
Sto
Woodspring
Sungersbery
Wrinton
Ragilbury
Chewret
Laurance veke
Perybridge
HVND
Puckston
PART OF BRENT
Butcombe
Nemnet
Worle
WINTERSTOAKE
Custok
Smaldon wood
HVND
Vbley
Weston vpon More
West Harty
Locking
Churchhill Roberrow
Blackdon
Coxton Martin
Banwell
Berrinton
Hutton
East H
Vphill
HVND
Shepcham
Bleydon
Chiston
Winscombe
Charterhouse
Locuston
Compton
Chedder rocke
The
Brayne
Ratclyffe
Axbridge
Mendip Hills
Hobbes passage
Chedder
This springe riseth so abundantly
Priddi
Limpsham
Bilsham
that it driveth 12 Mills within one
Rokesbridge
quarter of a mile from his head
Borrowgh
Wert
Hythe
WEILES &
East Brent
Baddesworth
Nyland hill
Radnestoke
HVND
Allerton
South Brent
Westbury
WELFOR
Barnham
Marcke
Wedmore
Wokey
Wokey hole
Brent Marshe
High bridge
Wike
Gedney more
BEMPS TON HVN DRED
Gedney
Polsha
Stokland Marshe
Meare poole
Aueland Island
GLASTONI
Otterhampton
CANING
Huntspill NORTH
Meare
Glassenburye
Hartlack bridge
Vi
land
Comwidg
Paulet
Bastian bridge
Stokgussey
Eiddington
PETHERTON
Peryton
Wollavington
Heth more
Shapwick
The Tore
Stowley
TON
Chilton
Downe end
Cussington
WHITELEIGH
Walton
Streete
Cannington
Wemdon
Baudrip
Chelton
Ashton
South Welton
Ouer Stowley
Sansford
HVNDRED
Stoke
Edington
Coripole
Charfynch
Bridgewater
Chedsey
Grendon
Iuythorne
holt HVNDRE
Spaxton
Durlay
Sutton
Morlynch
Busley
Enmore
Huntworth
Weston
Sedege more
HVNDRED
West Carlton
Brumfeld
Goteburst
Quenes more
Middledey
Kyewqdon
North petherto
Audre
Petherton parke
Audre more
Cumpton Dundo
East Carlton
eleston
Kingston
N More
Highham
ANDRESFEILD
Anthony
Michaels Burro
Lengham
ard

Bibliography

Primary

Samuel Dassell's account of Monmouth's landing (Somerset and Dorset Notes and Queries, Vol. XXVIII, 1961.)

Nathaniel Wade's Narrative.

The Battle of Sedgemoor – The Revd. Andrew Paschall's second narrative from Notes and Queries for Somerset and Dorset, Vol. XXVIII edited by T. V. Hunt, B.A. and Philip N. Dawe, 1961.

A copy of an account by Andrew Paschall found at Messrs. Hoare's Bank in 1939 now hanging in Westonzoyland Church, Somerset.

Also in the same Church an account of *The Fight that was in Longmoor*, together with a copy of *The Battle of Sedgemoor, 1685.*

The Western Rebellion, by Richard Locke, printed and sold by H. Norris, 1782.

In the Philpot Museum, Lyme Regis:
The Hewling Manuscript, 1685-90, from the Cromwell Family Papers.
Letter from Gregory Alford, Mayor of Lyme Regis, to King James II on 11th June, 1685, informing him of the landing of Monmouth.
An account for entertaining Judge Jeffreys and his fellow Judges on the Commission when they entered Lyme Regis in September, 1685.

Secondary

Macaulay, Thomas Babington. *The History of England* Vols. 1 to 4, Dent's Everyman Library.

Samuel Pepys' *Diary*. Pub. J. M. Dent & Sons Ltd., 1930.

Roberts, George. *The Life, Progresses and Rebellion of James, Duke of Monmouth* Vol. 1 & 2. Pub. Longman, Brown, Green & Longmans, 1844.

Wigfield, W. M. *The Monmouth Rebellion*. Moonraker Press 1980.

Bevin, Bryan. *James, Duke of Monmouth*. Robert Hale & Co. 1973.

Chevenix Trench, C. *The Western Rising. An Account of Monmouth's Rebellion*. Longmans, 1969.

Little, Bryan. *The Monmouth Episode*. Werner Laurie, 1956.

Young and Adair. *Hastings to Culloden*. G. Bell & Sons Ltd. 1964.

Earle, Peter. *Monmouth's Rebels*. Weidenfeld & Nicholson, 1977.

Wyndham, Violet. *The Protestant Duke*. Weidenfeld & Nicholson, 1976.

Clifton, Robin. *The Last Popular Rebellion*. Maurice Temple Smith, 1984.

Baines, Anna. *The Monmouth Rebellion in Wells*. Wells Museum, Somerset, 1985.

King, E. *Old Times Revisited*. Shurlock. 2nd edition. 1900.

Parry, Sir Edward. *The Bloody Assize*. Ernest Benn, 1929.

Schofield, Semour. *Jeffreys of 'The Bloody Assizes'*. Thornton Butterworth, 1937.

Keeton, G. W. *Trial for Treason*. Macdonald, 1959.

Helm, P. J. *Jeffreys*. Robert Hale, 1966.

Opposite: Contemporary map of the Sedgemoor area, by John Speed.

Index